This coloring book belongs to:

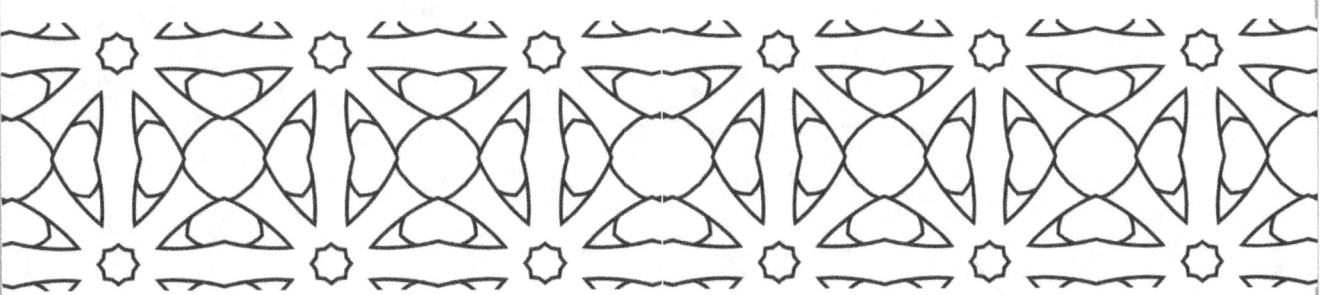

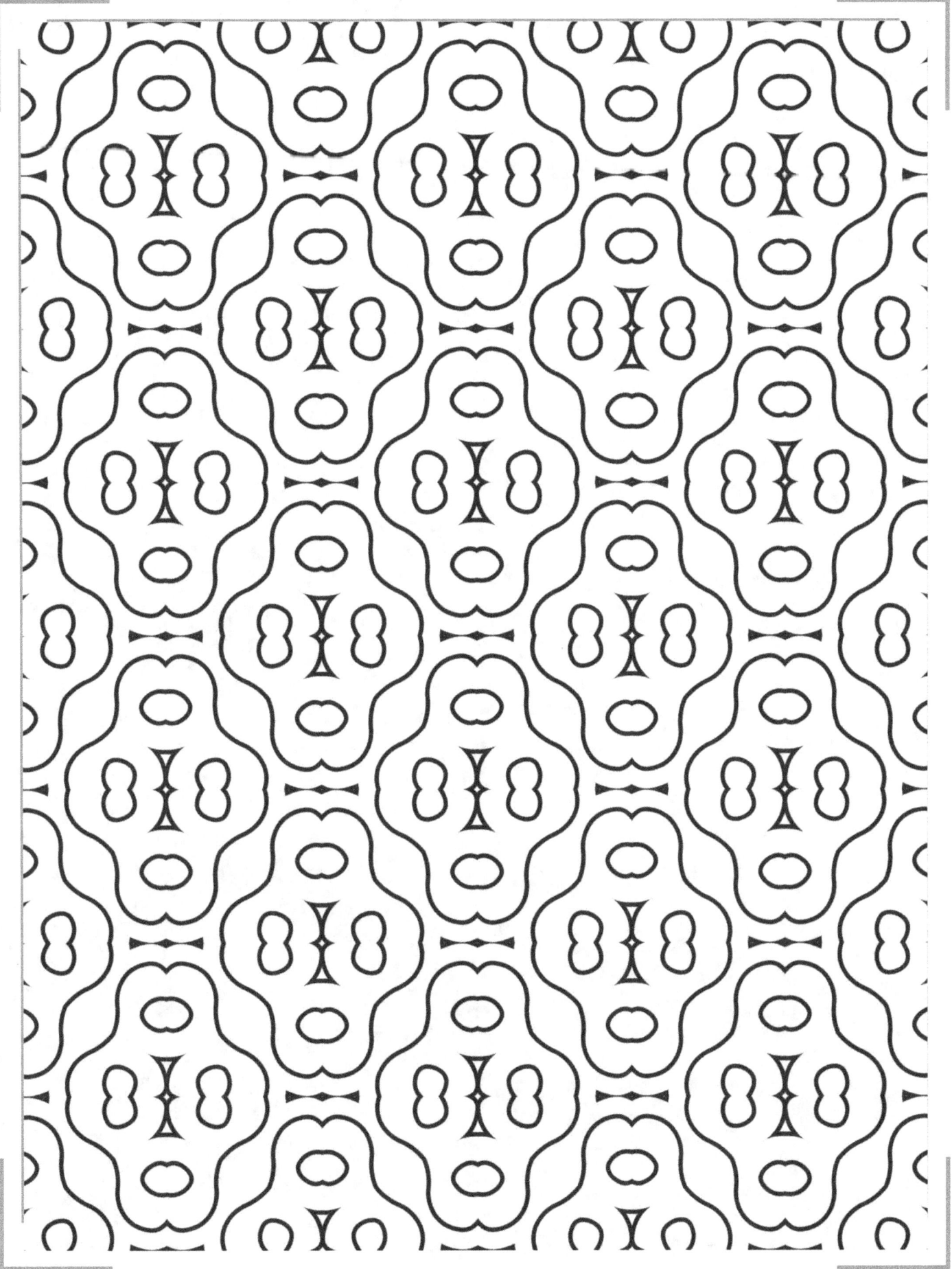

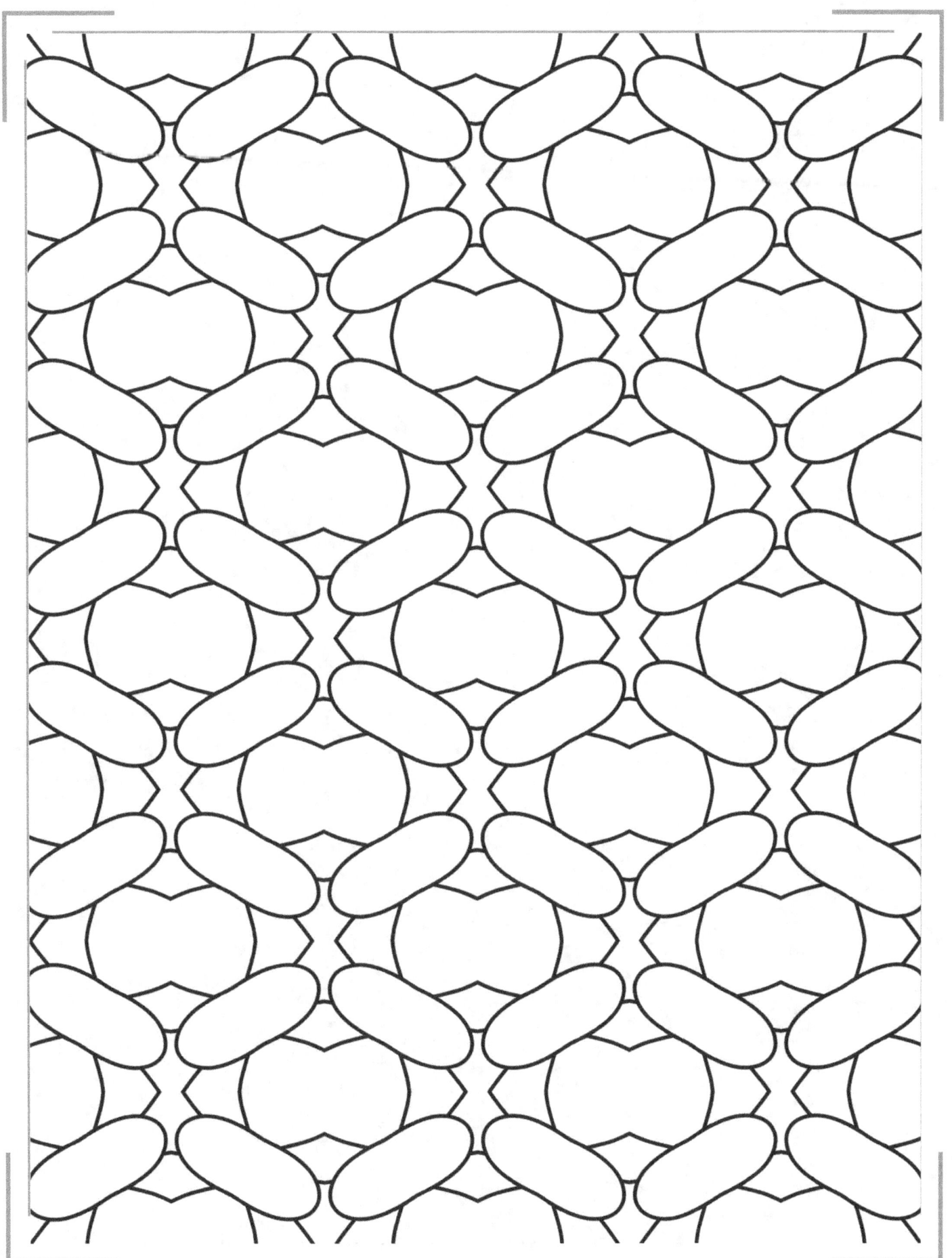

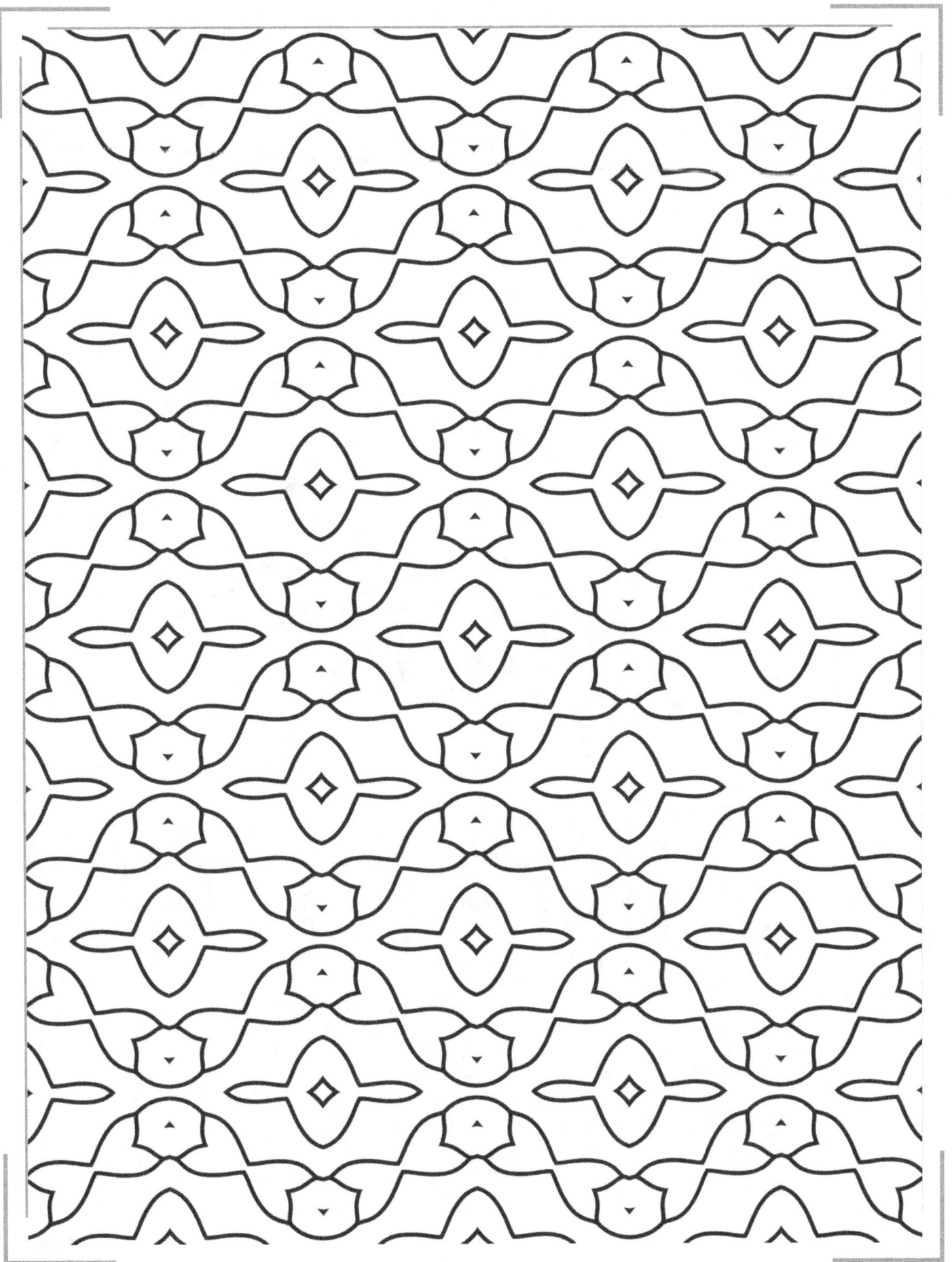

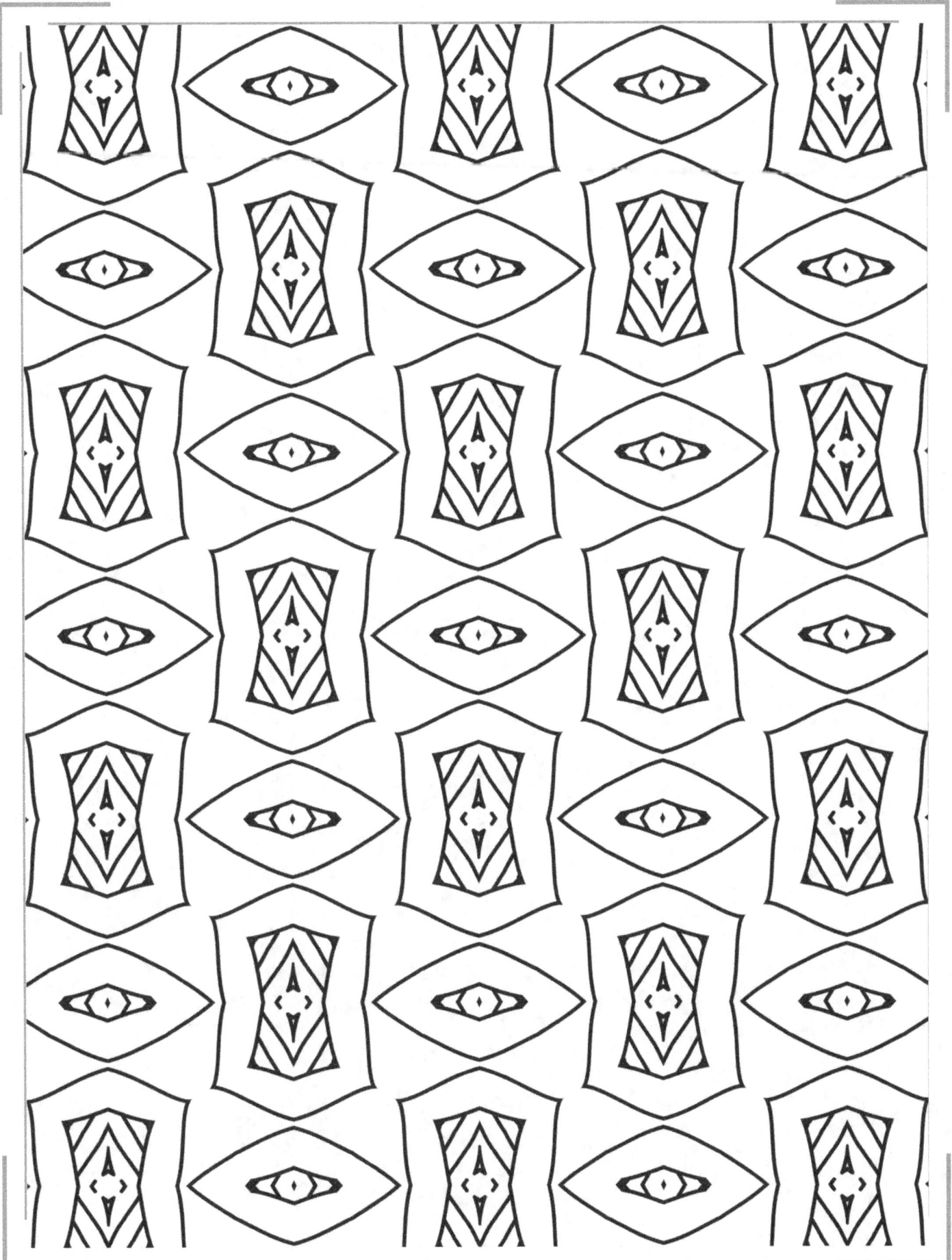

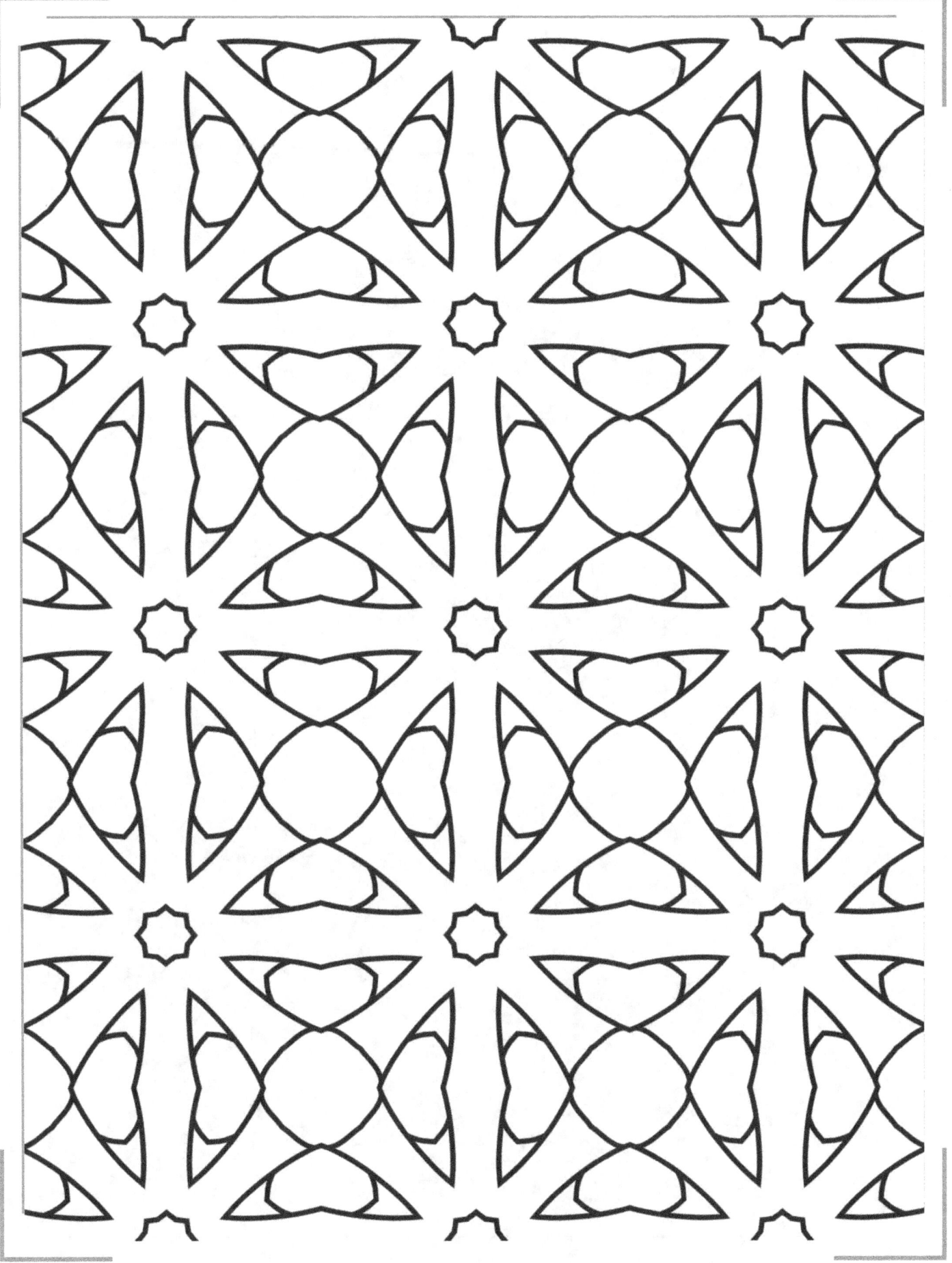

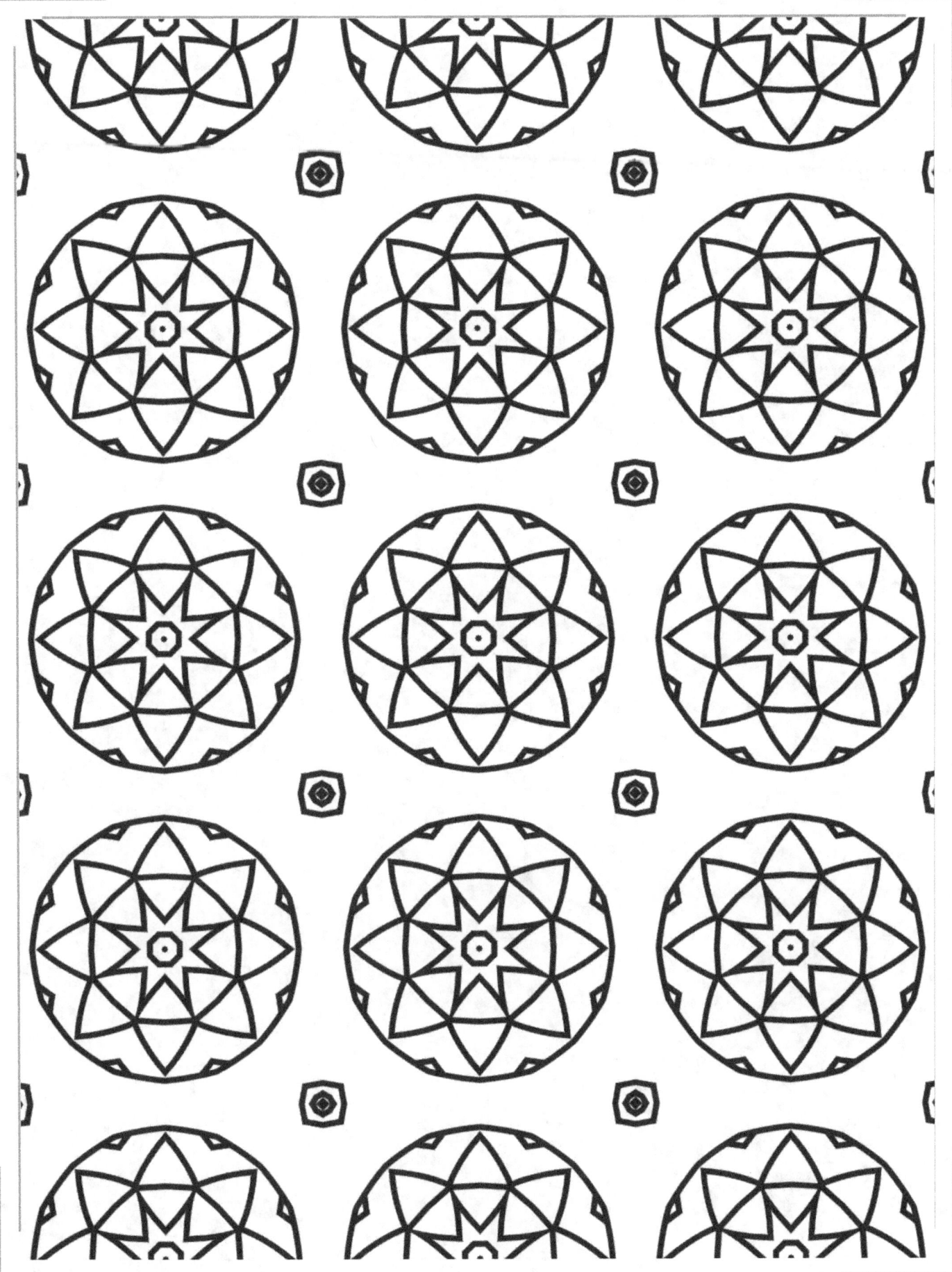

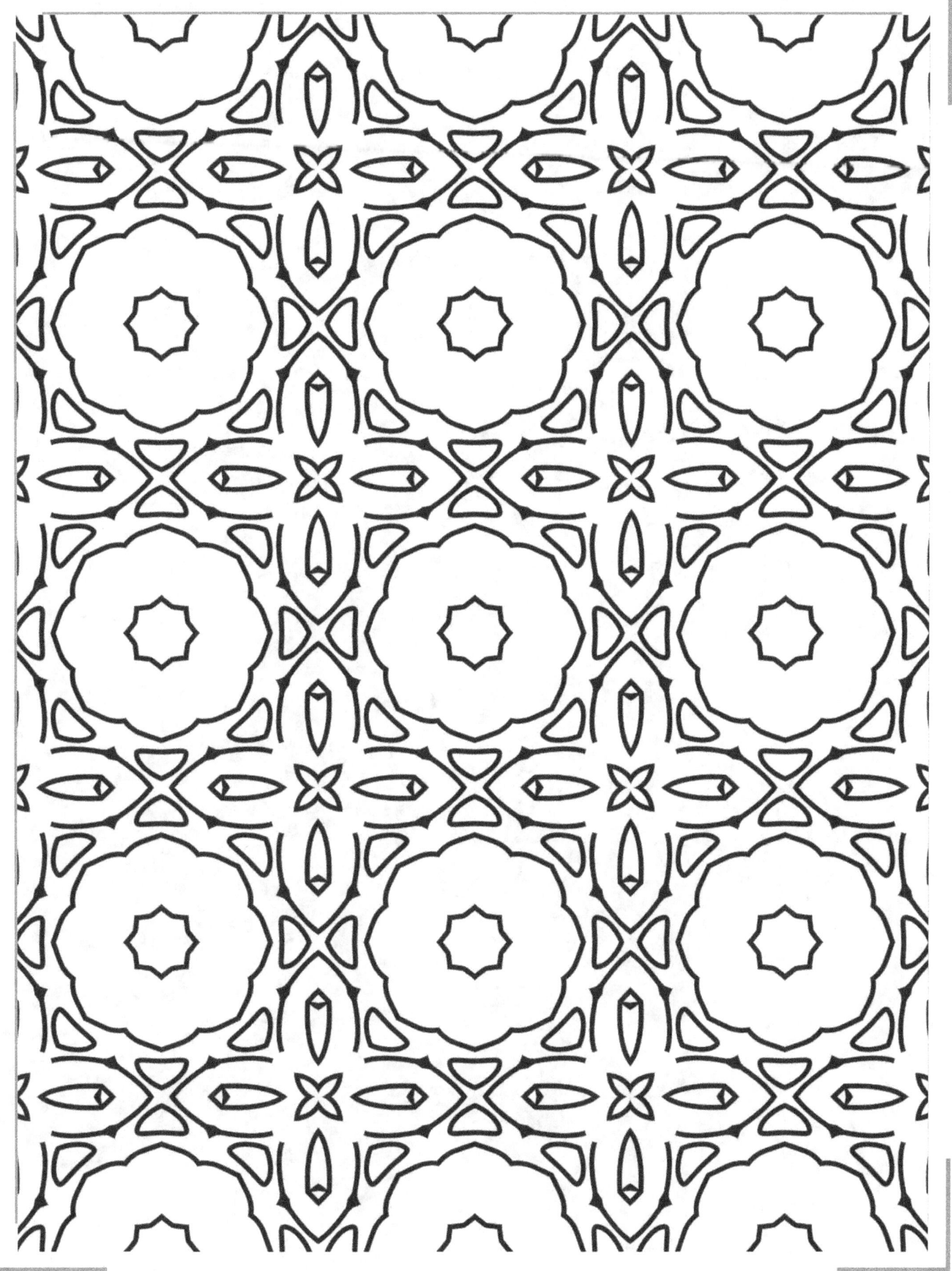

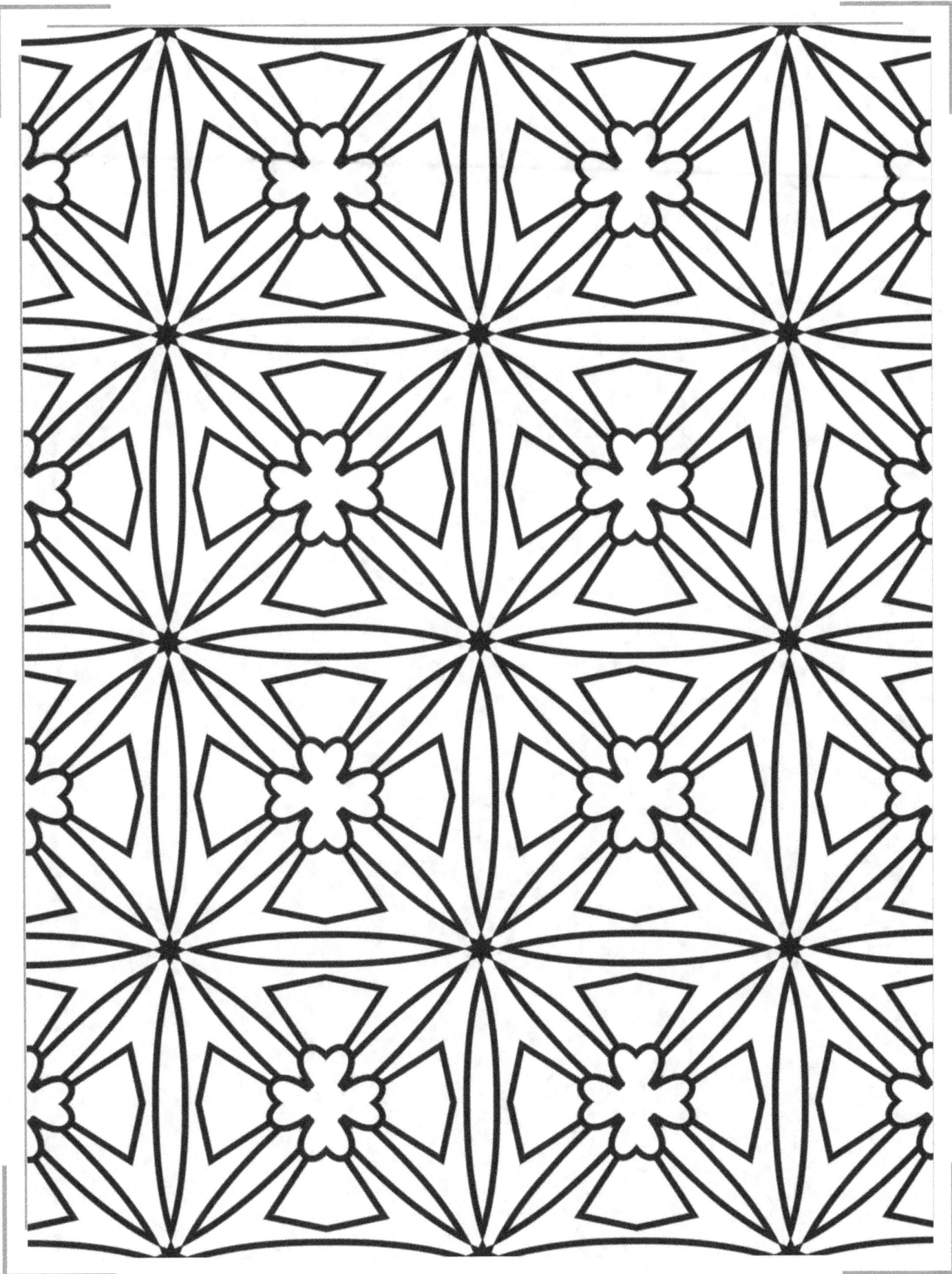

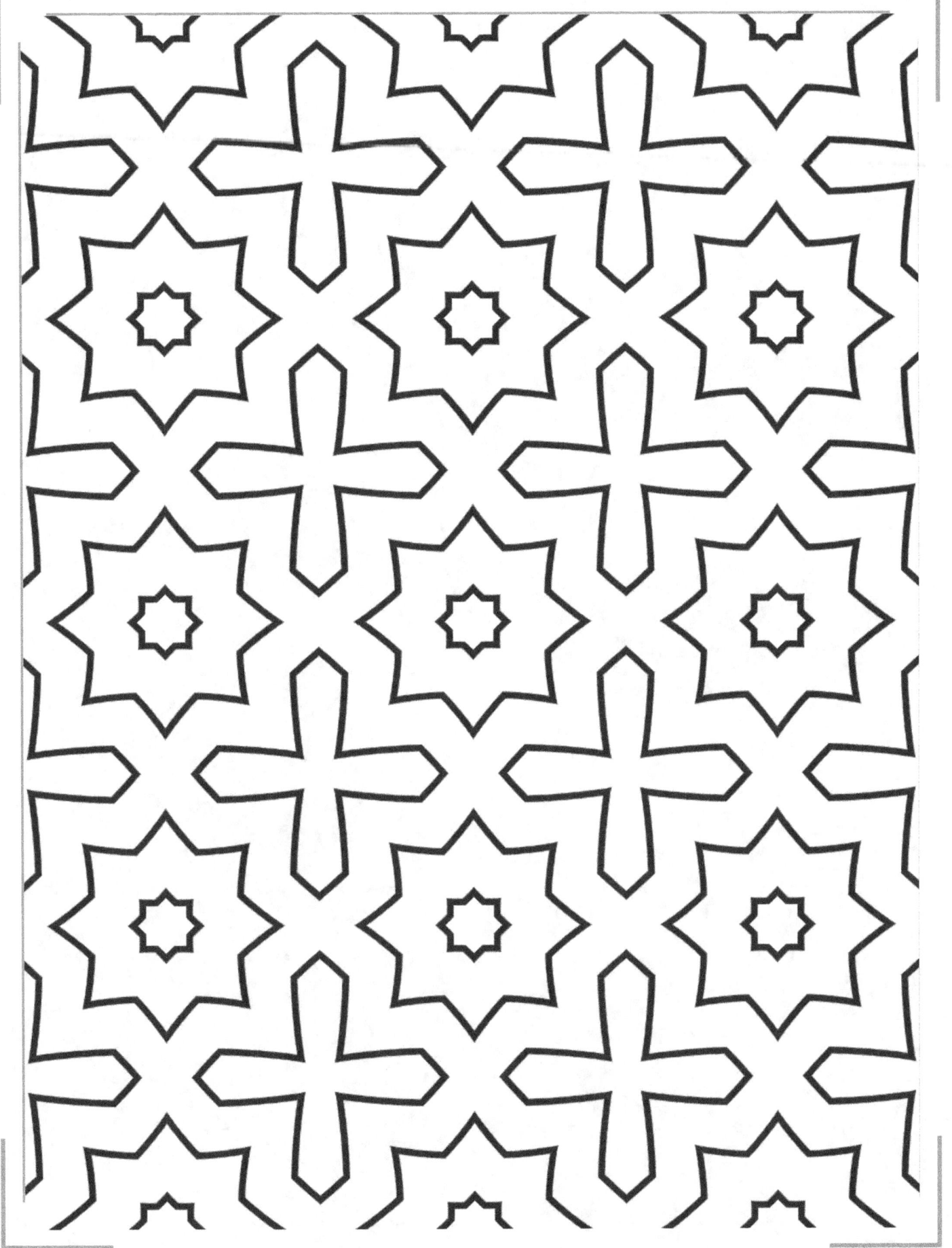

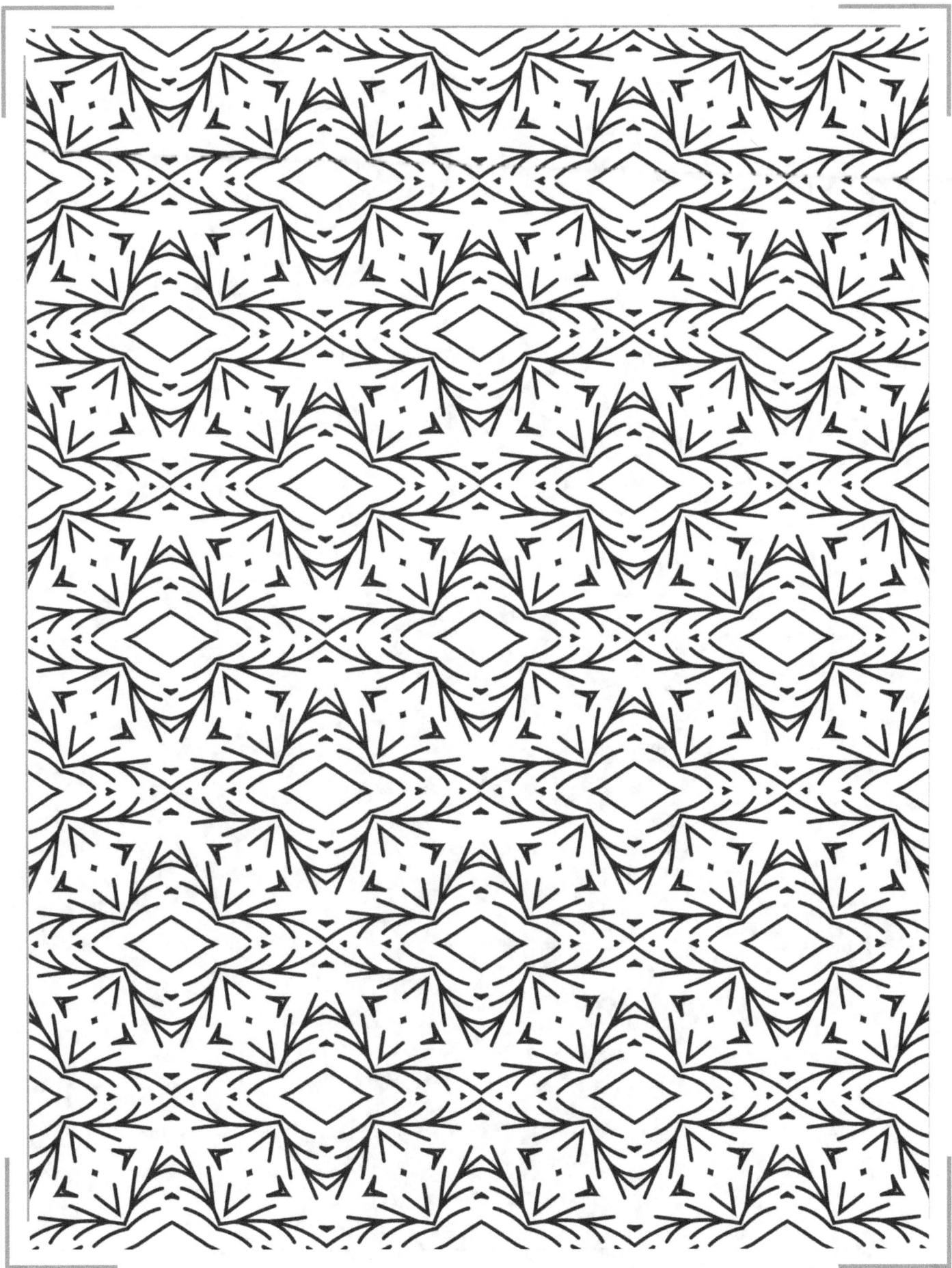

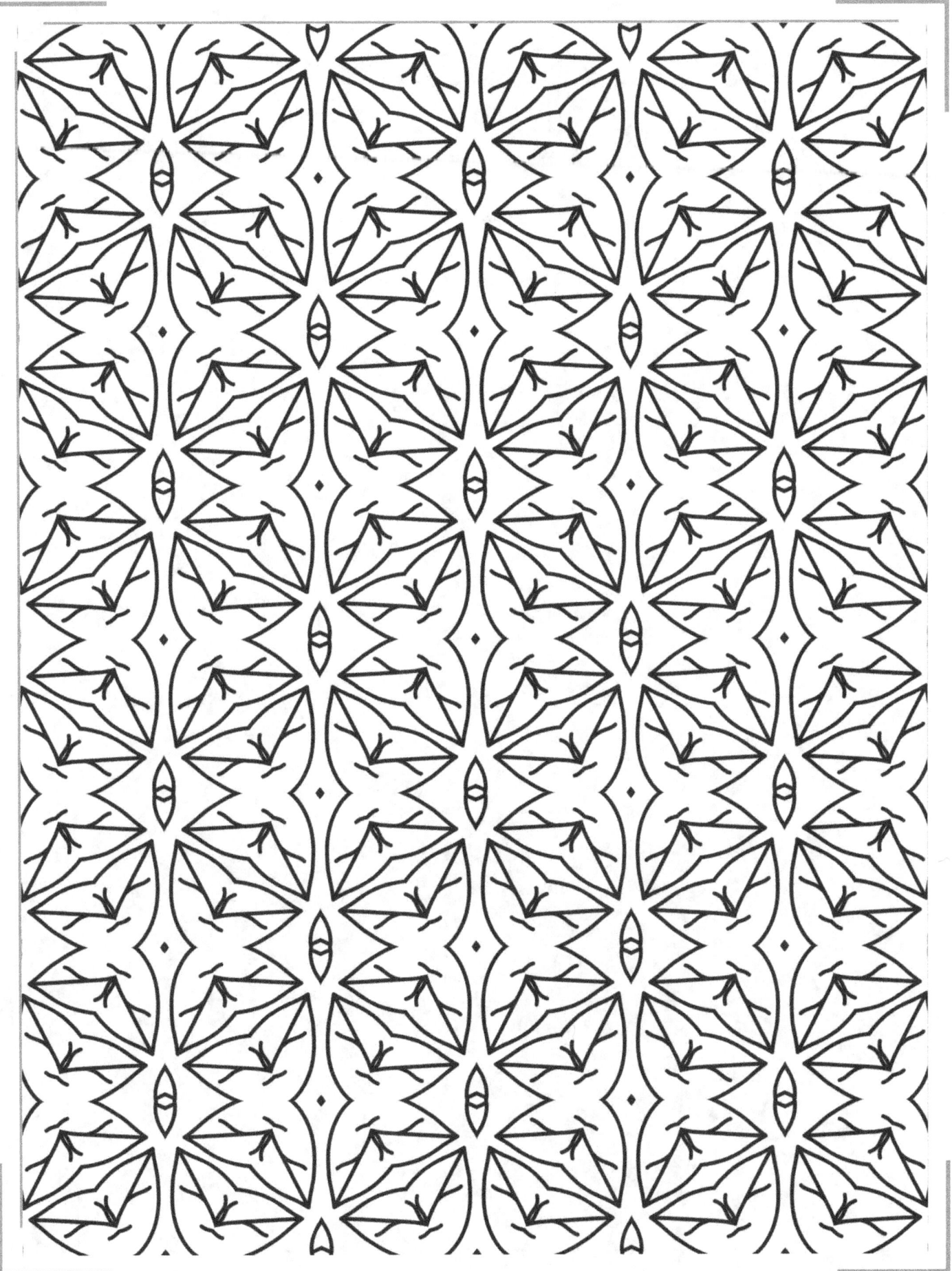

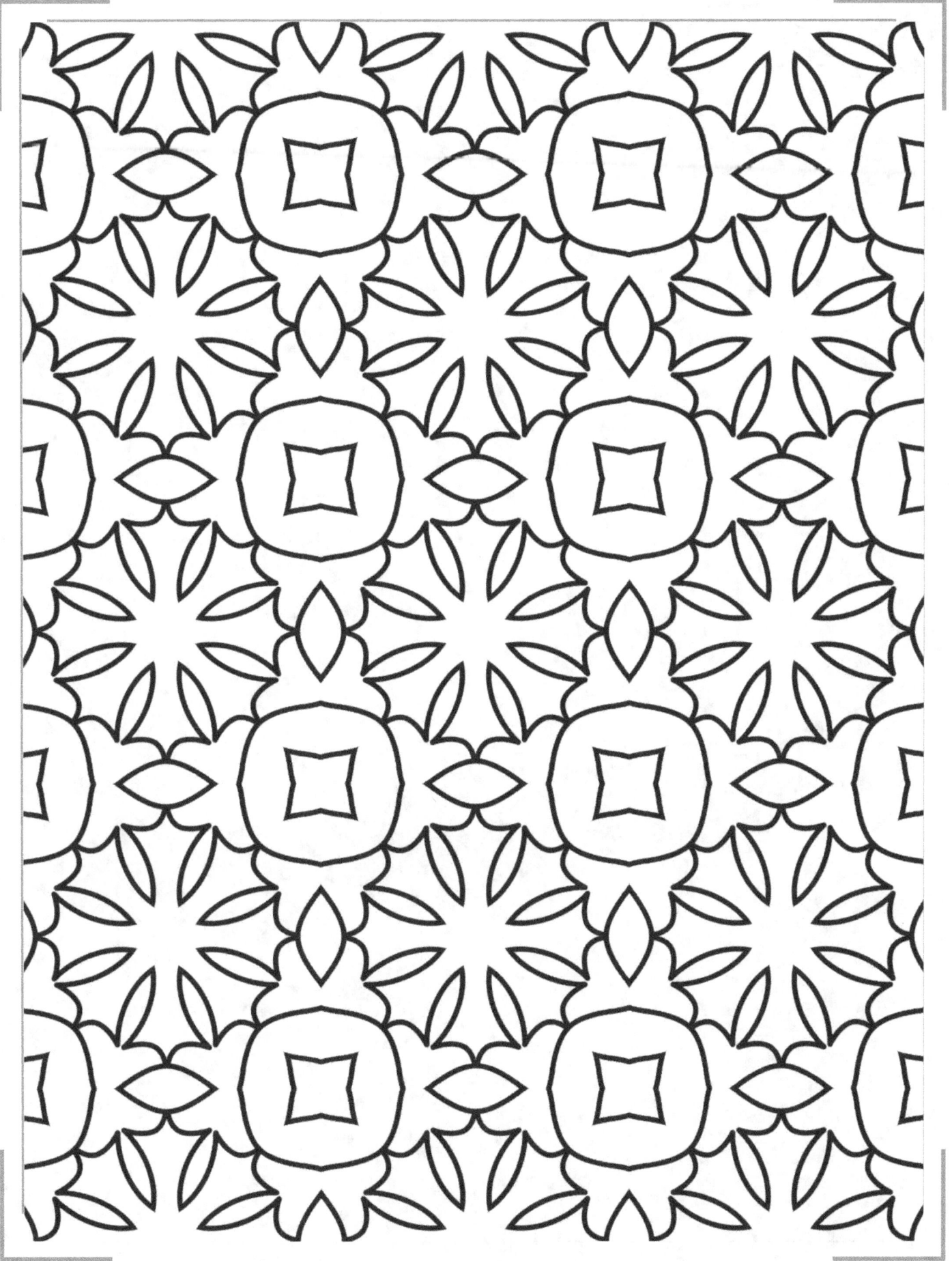

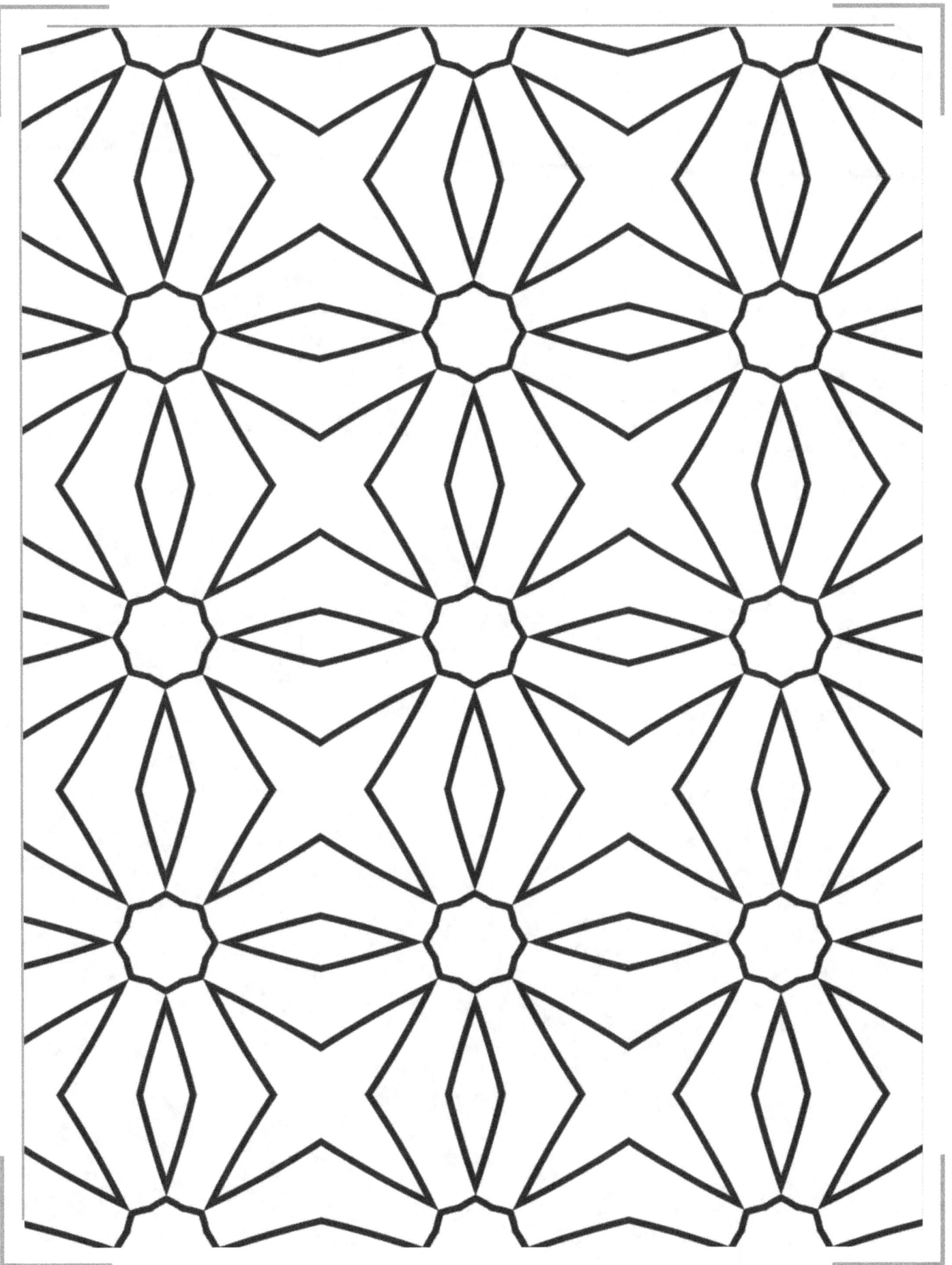

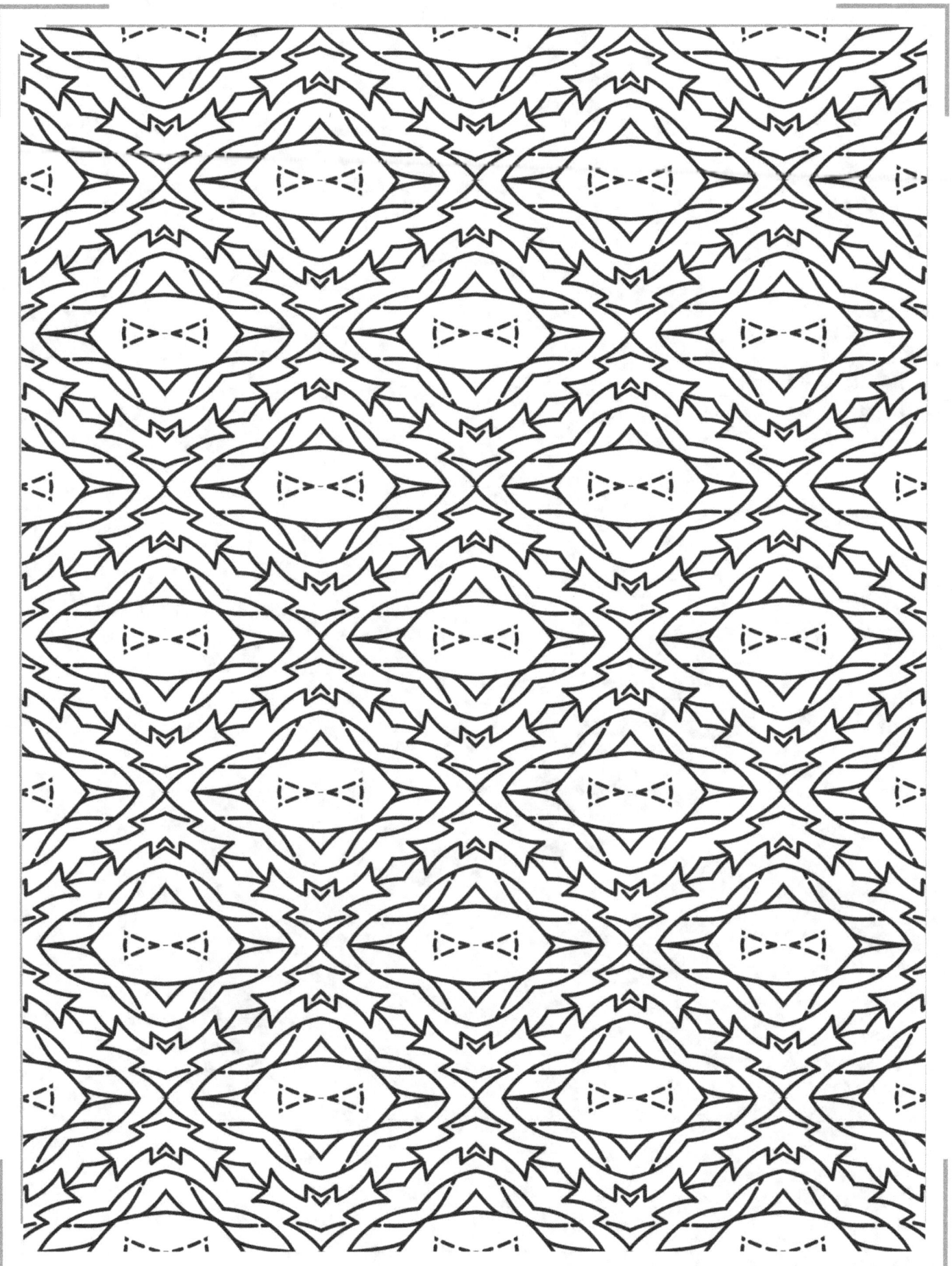

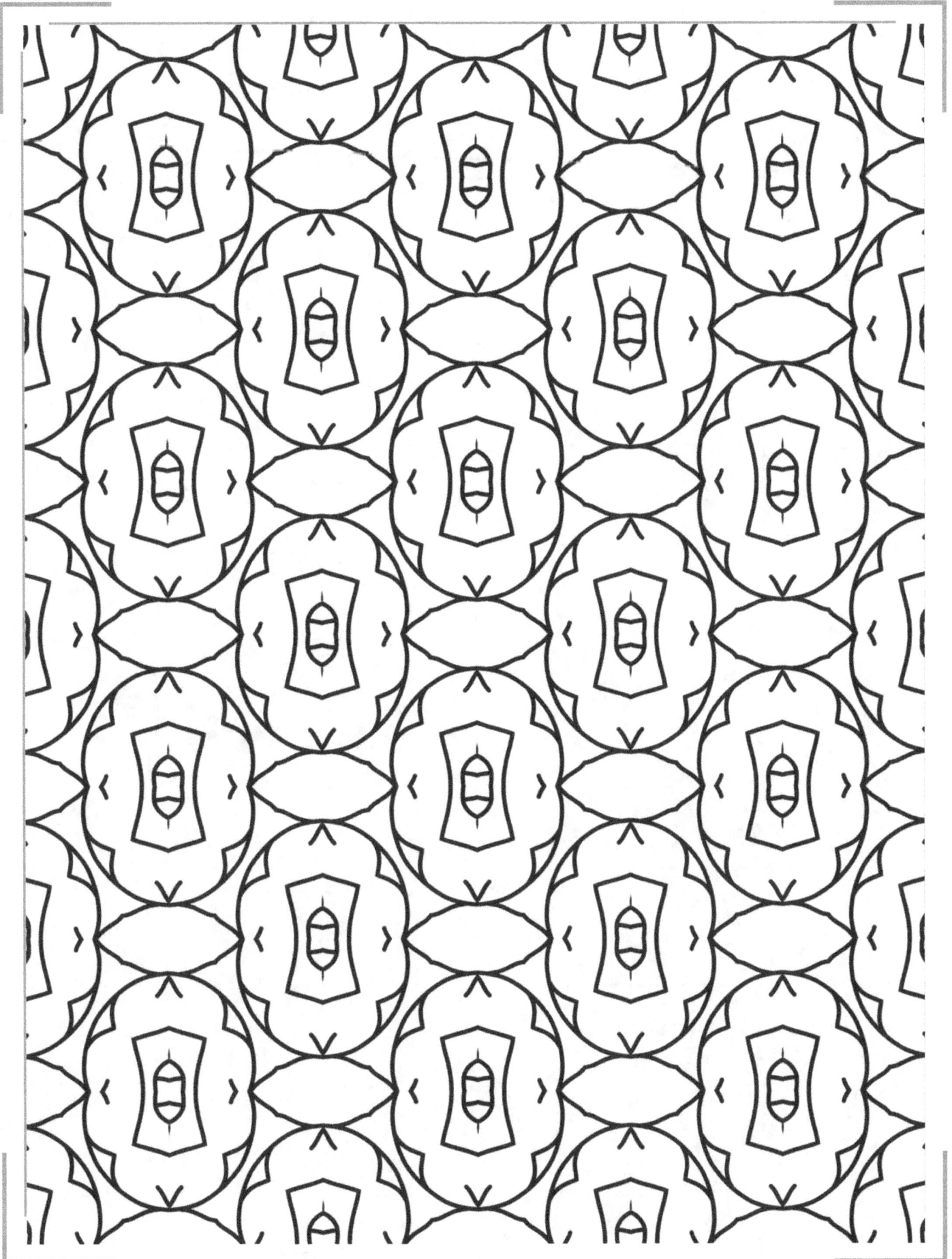

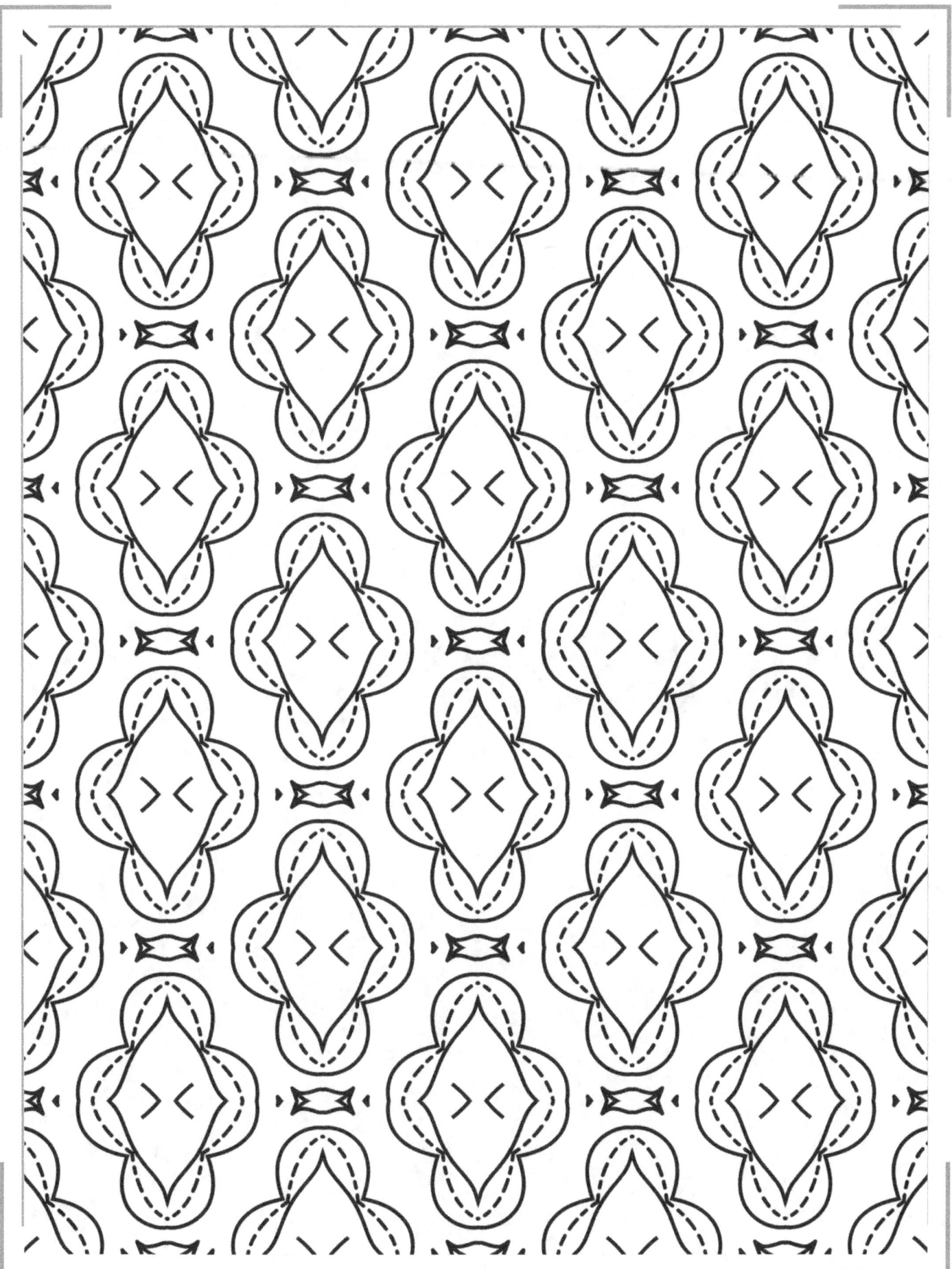

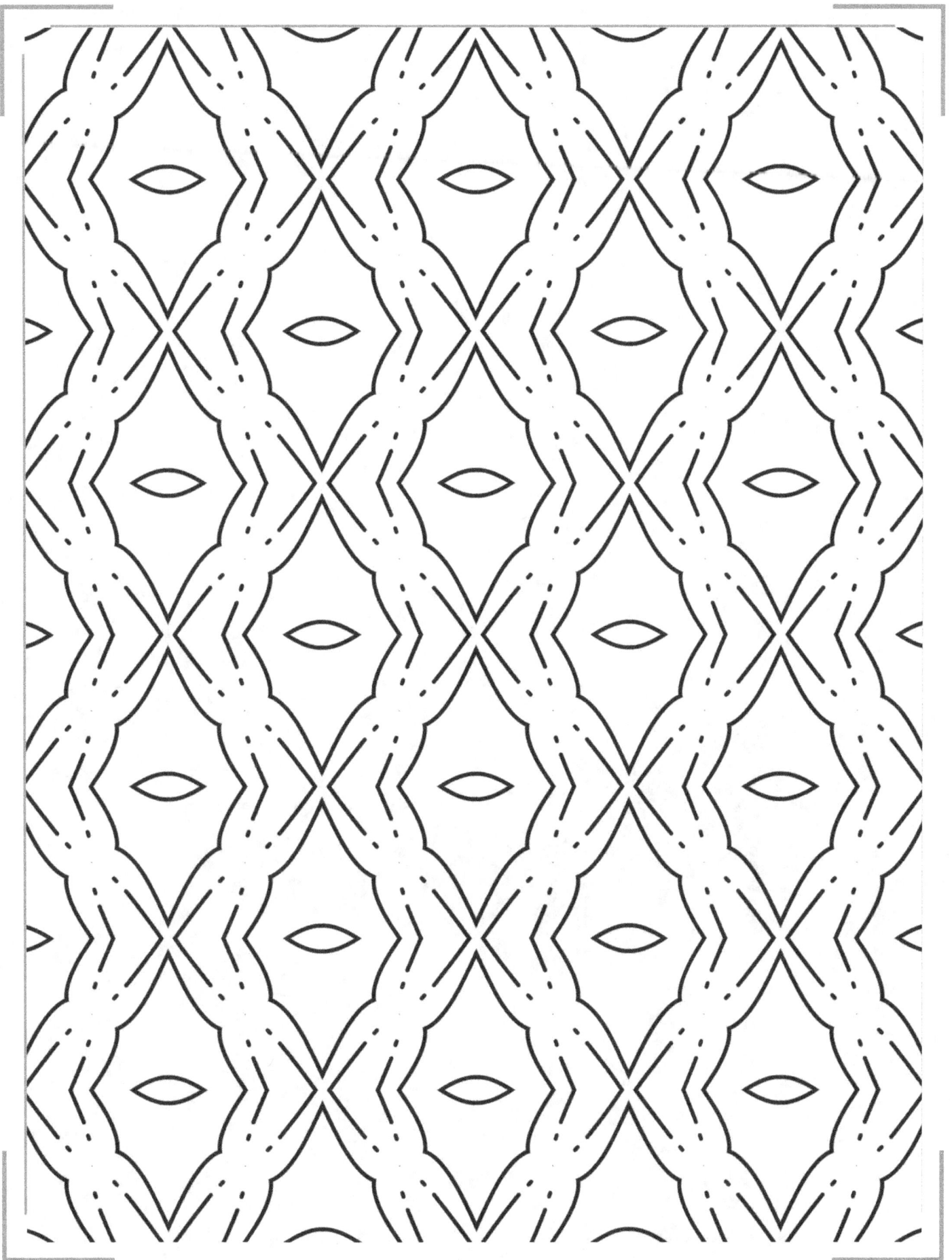

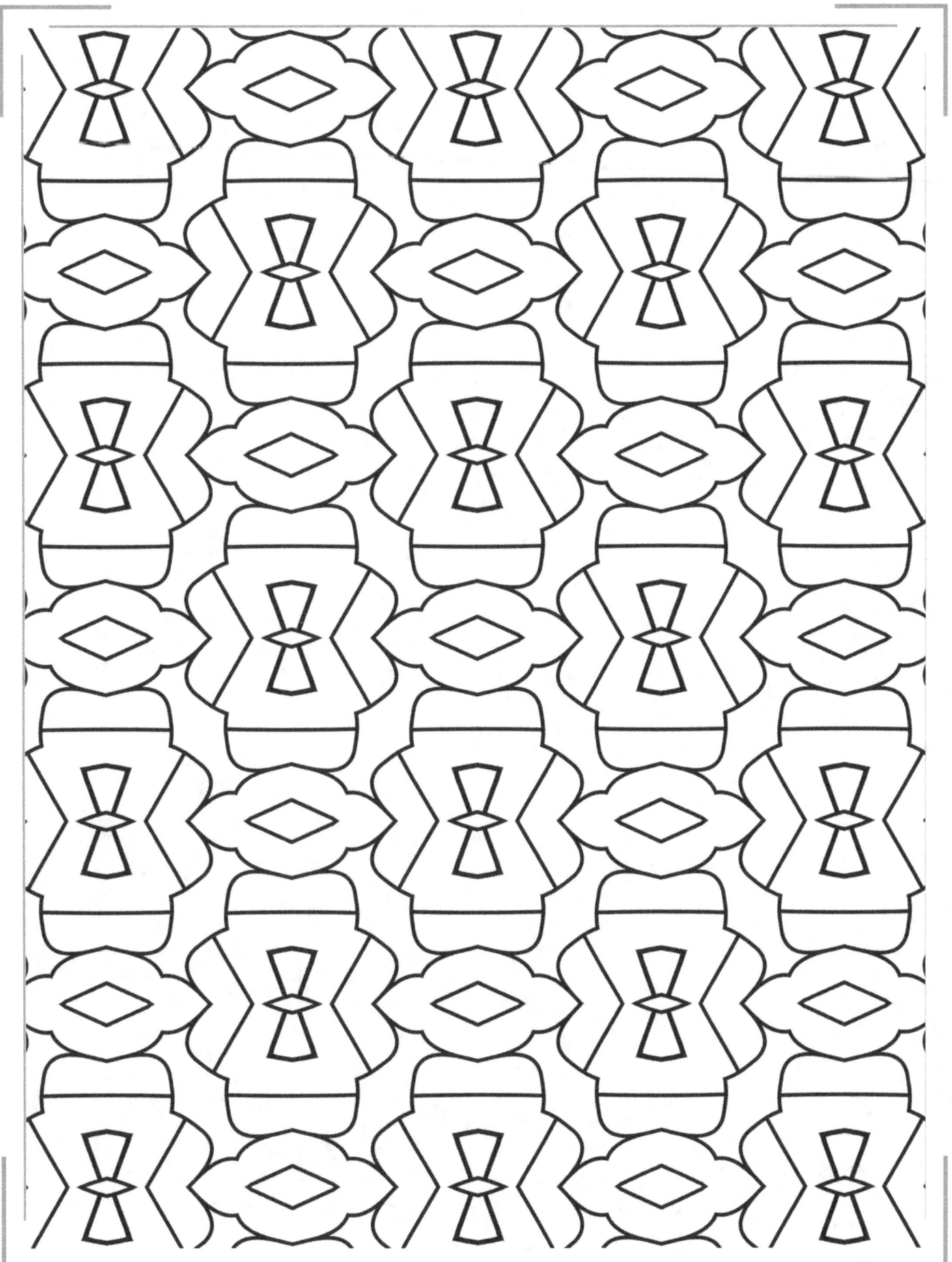

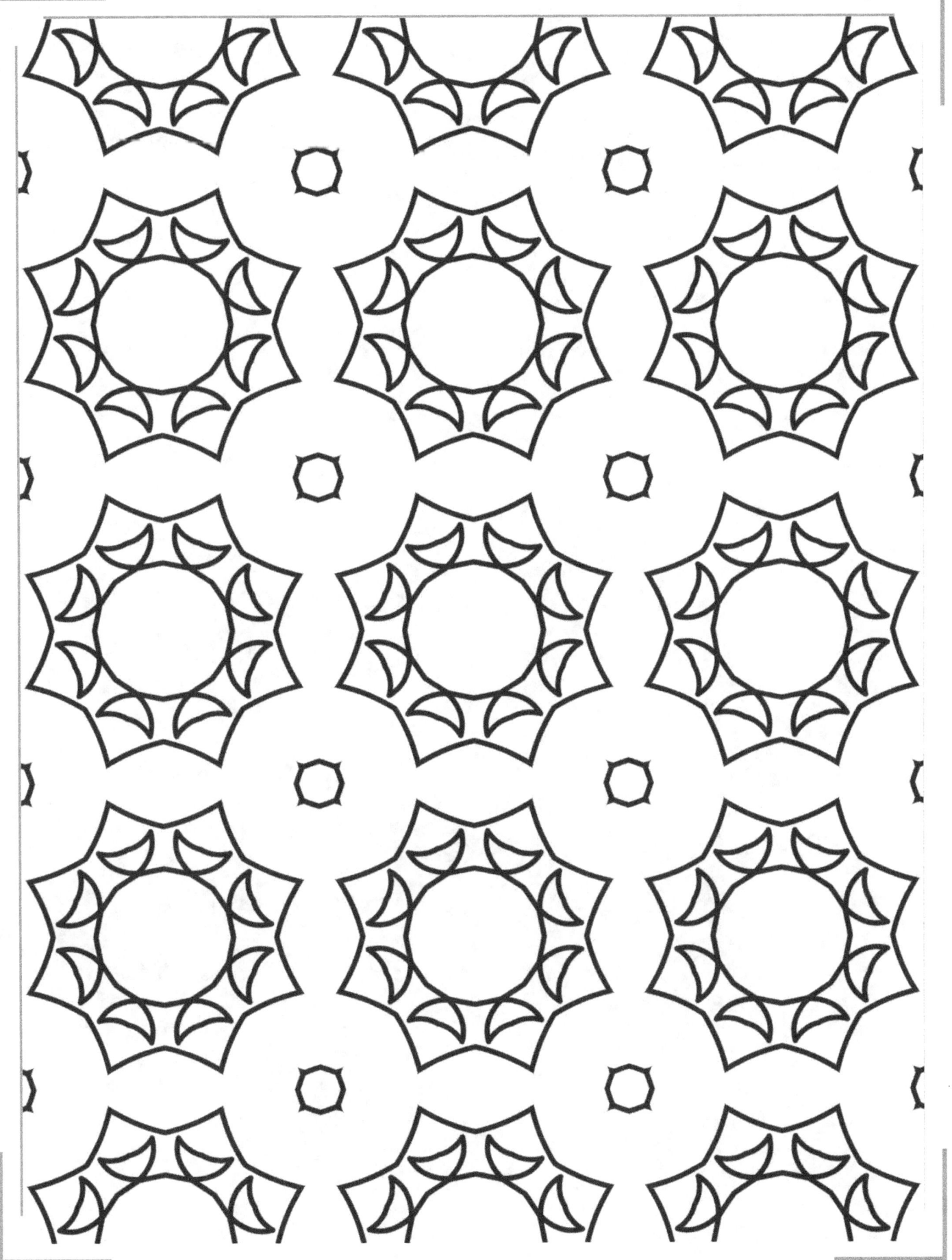

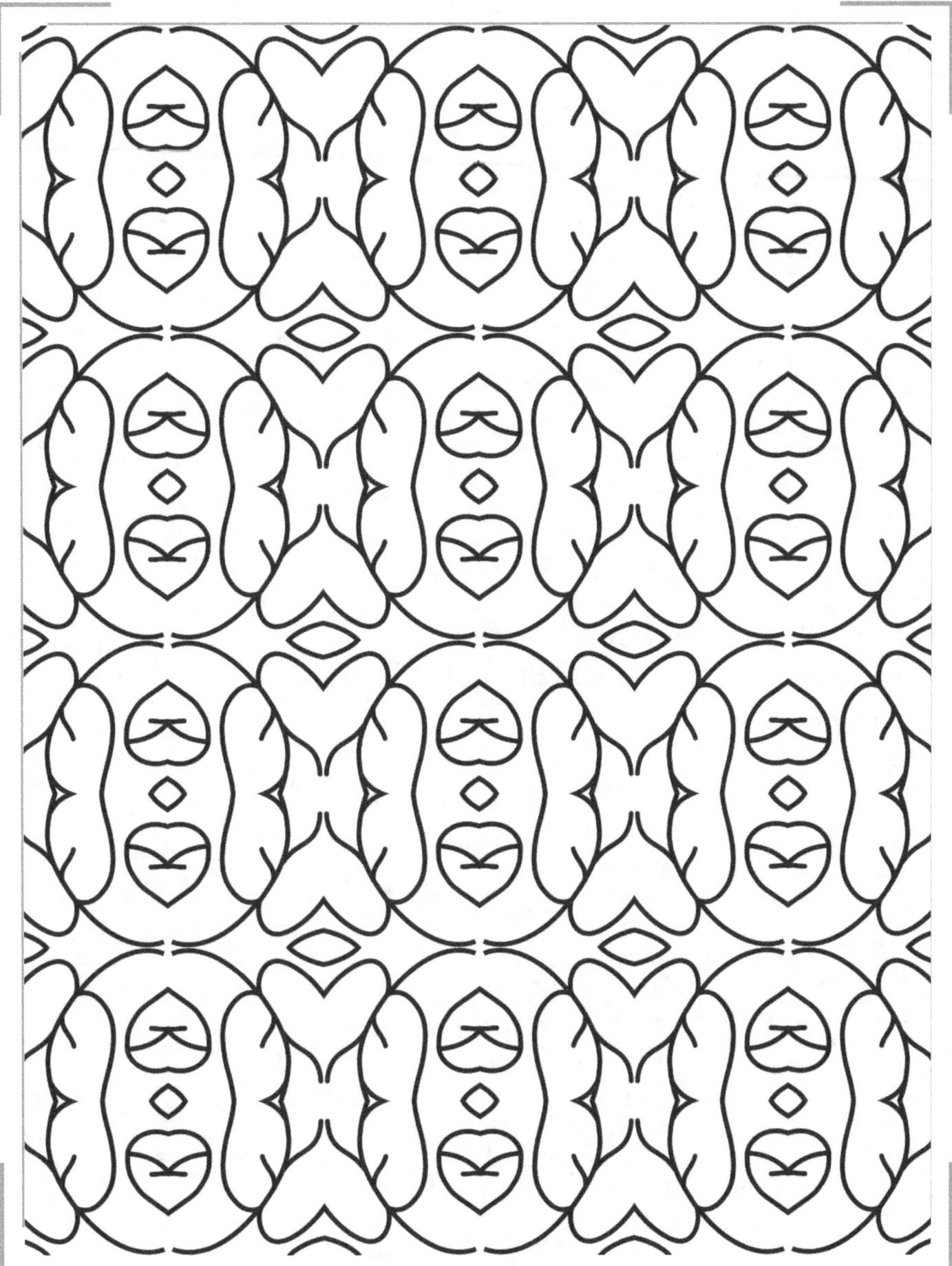

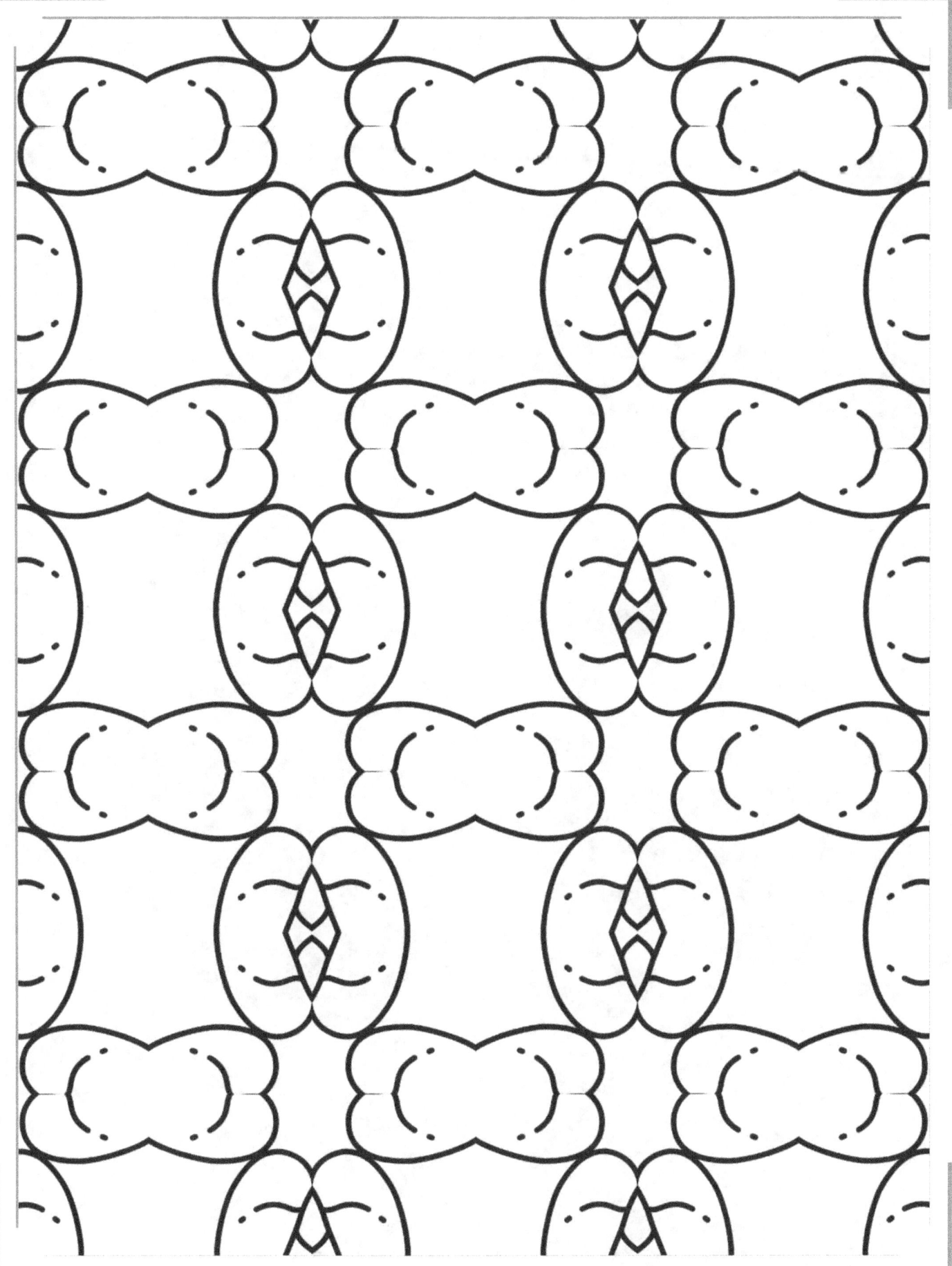

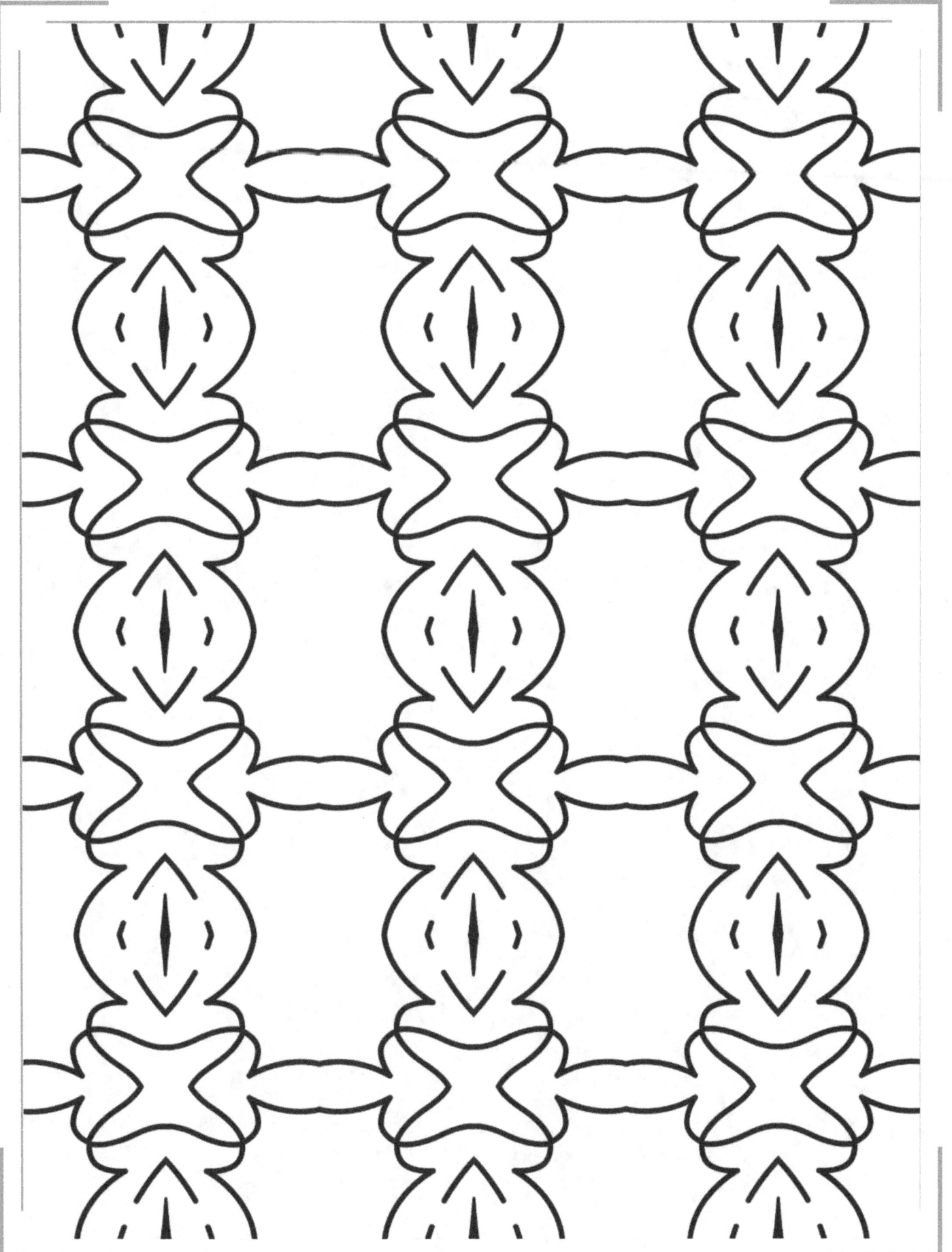

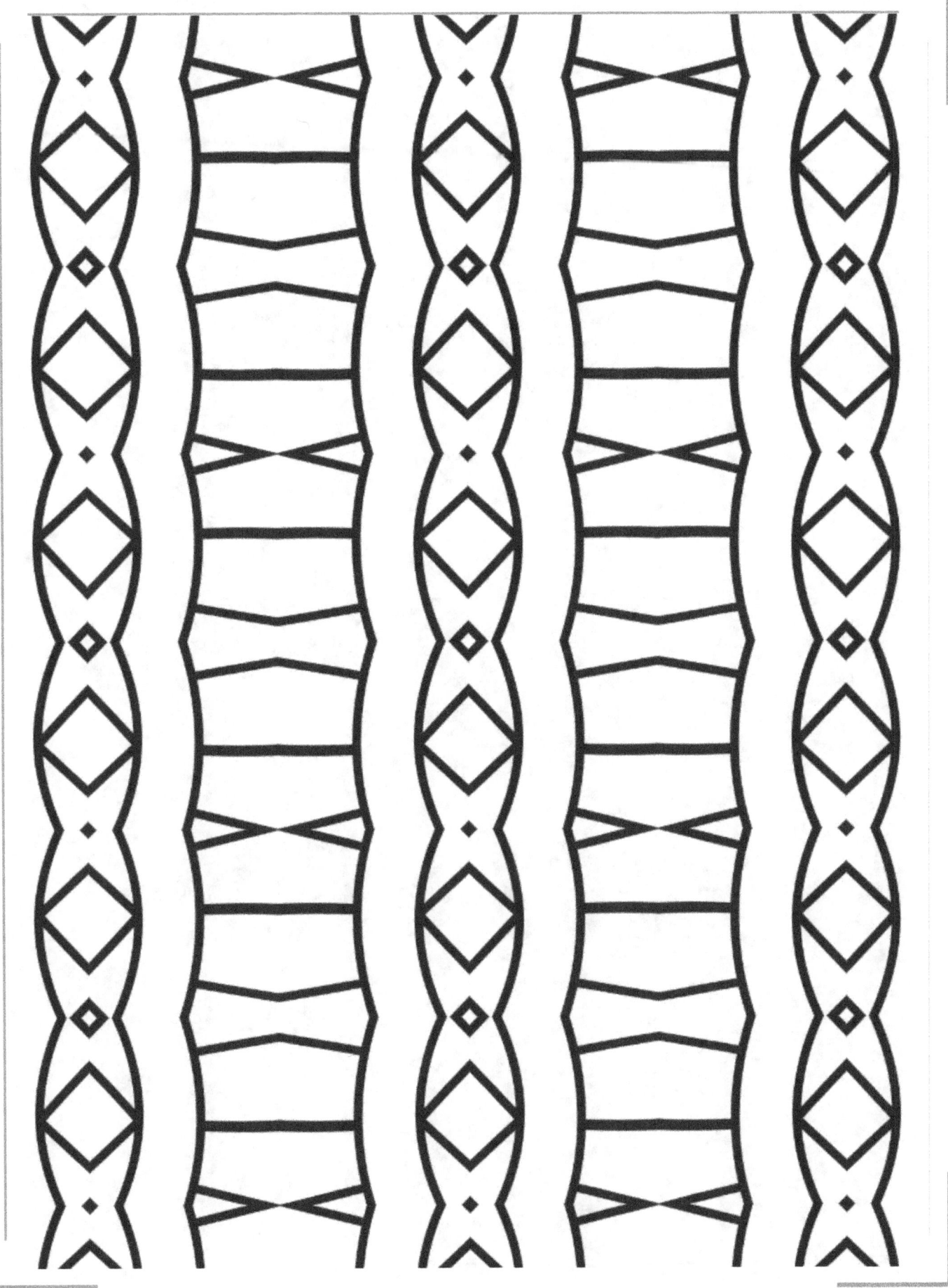

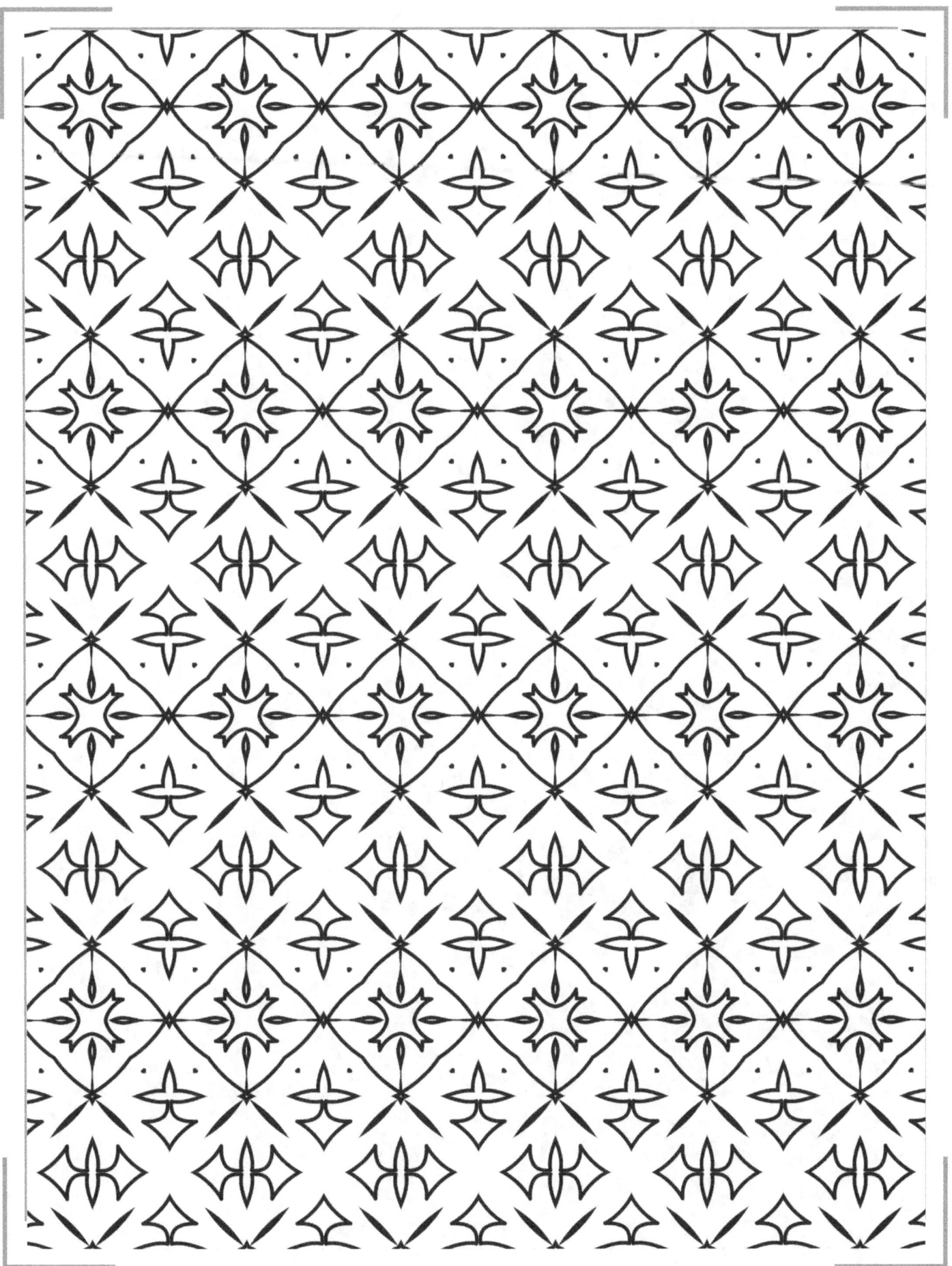

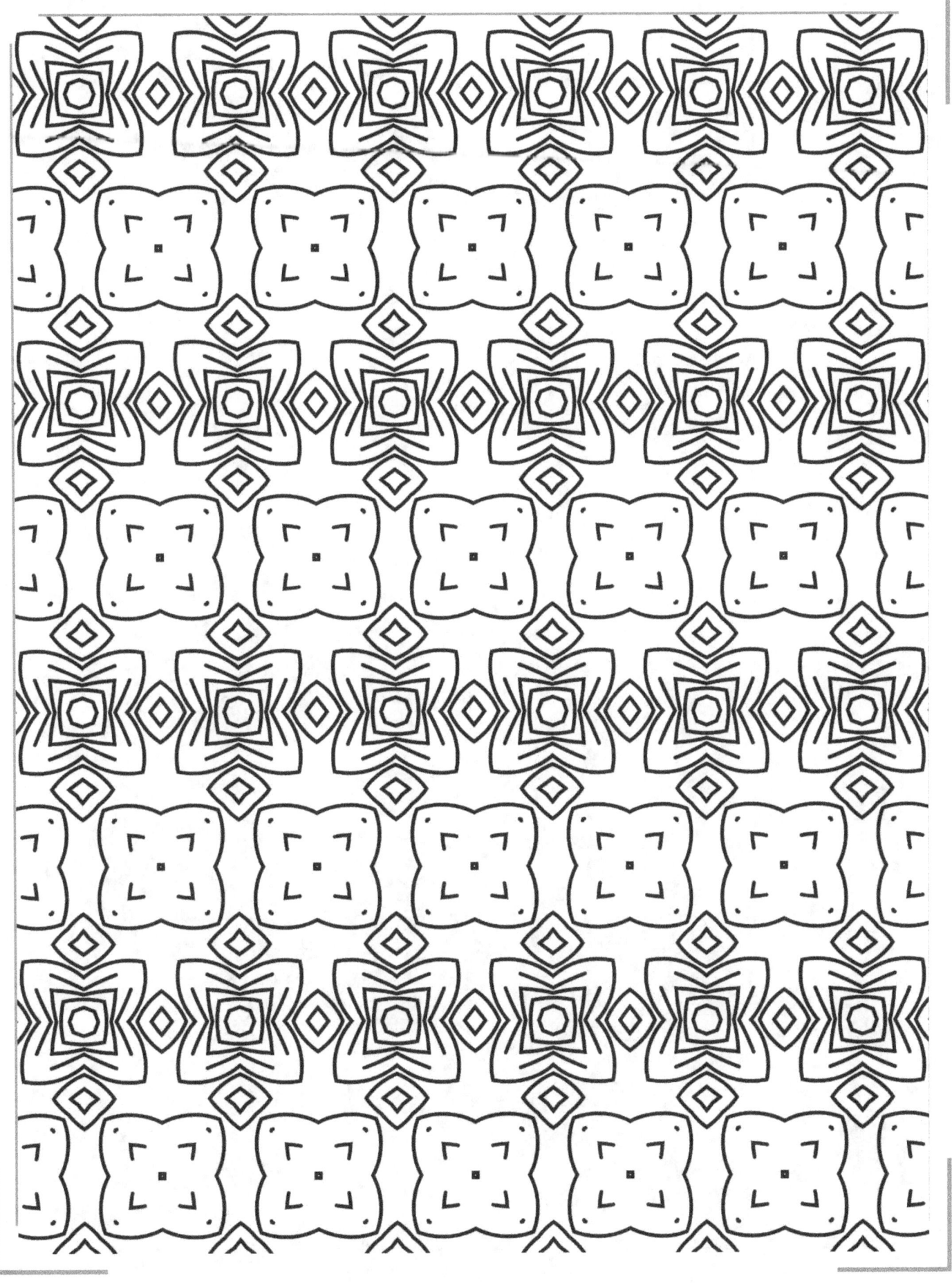

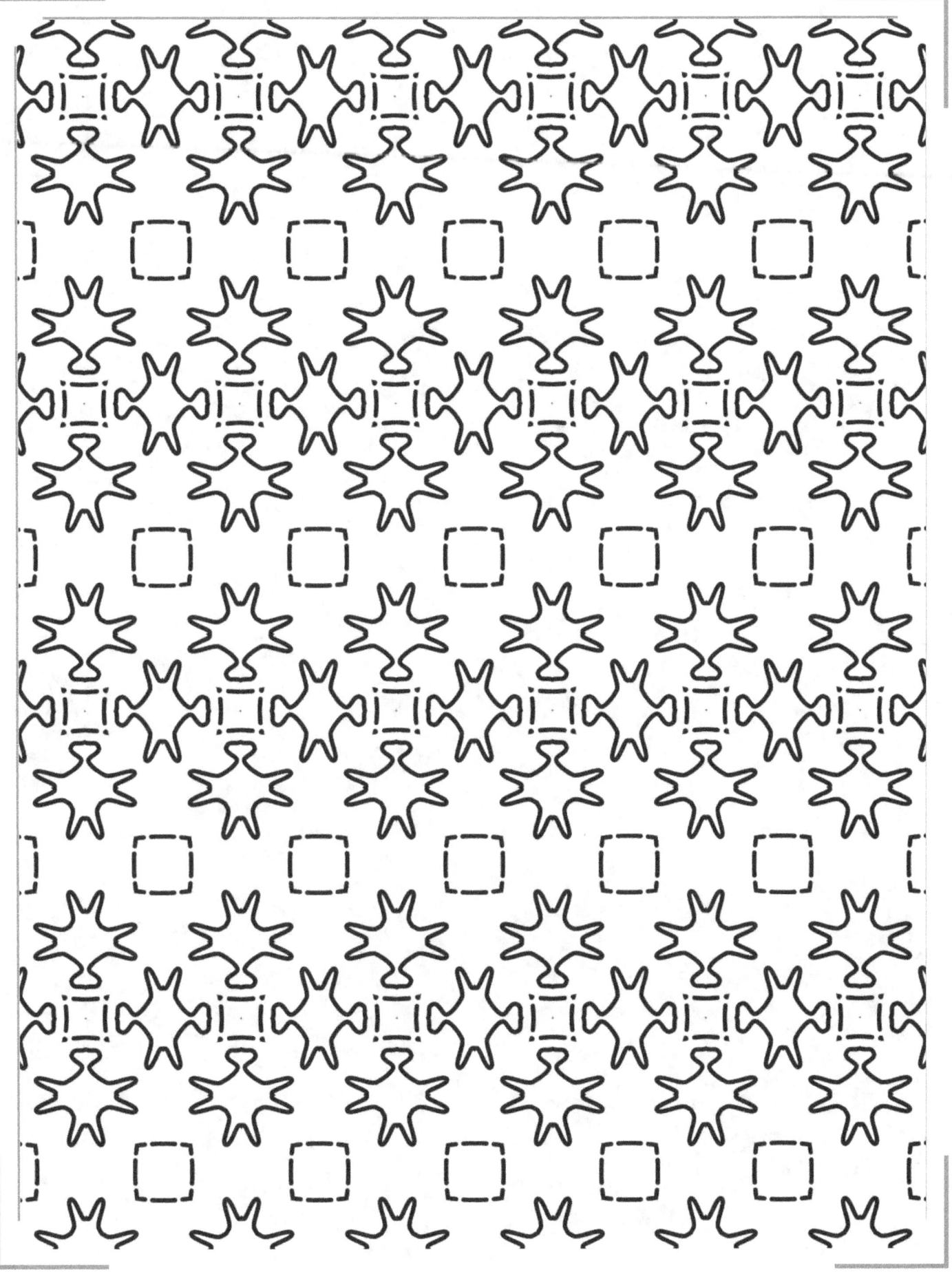

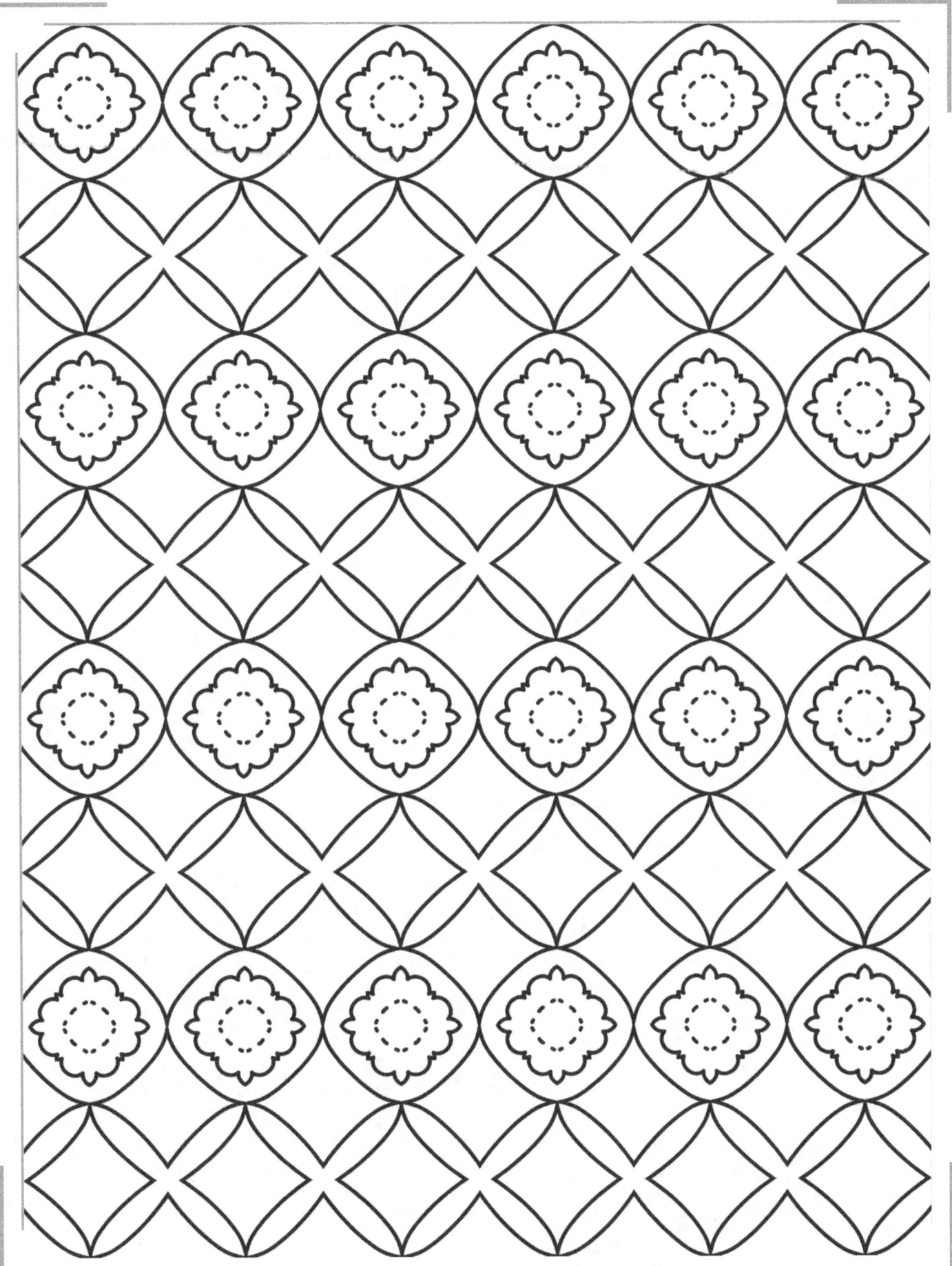

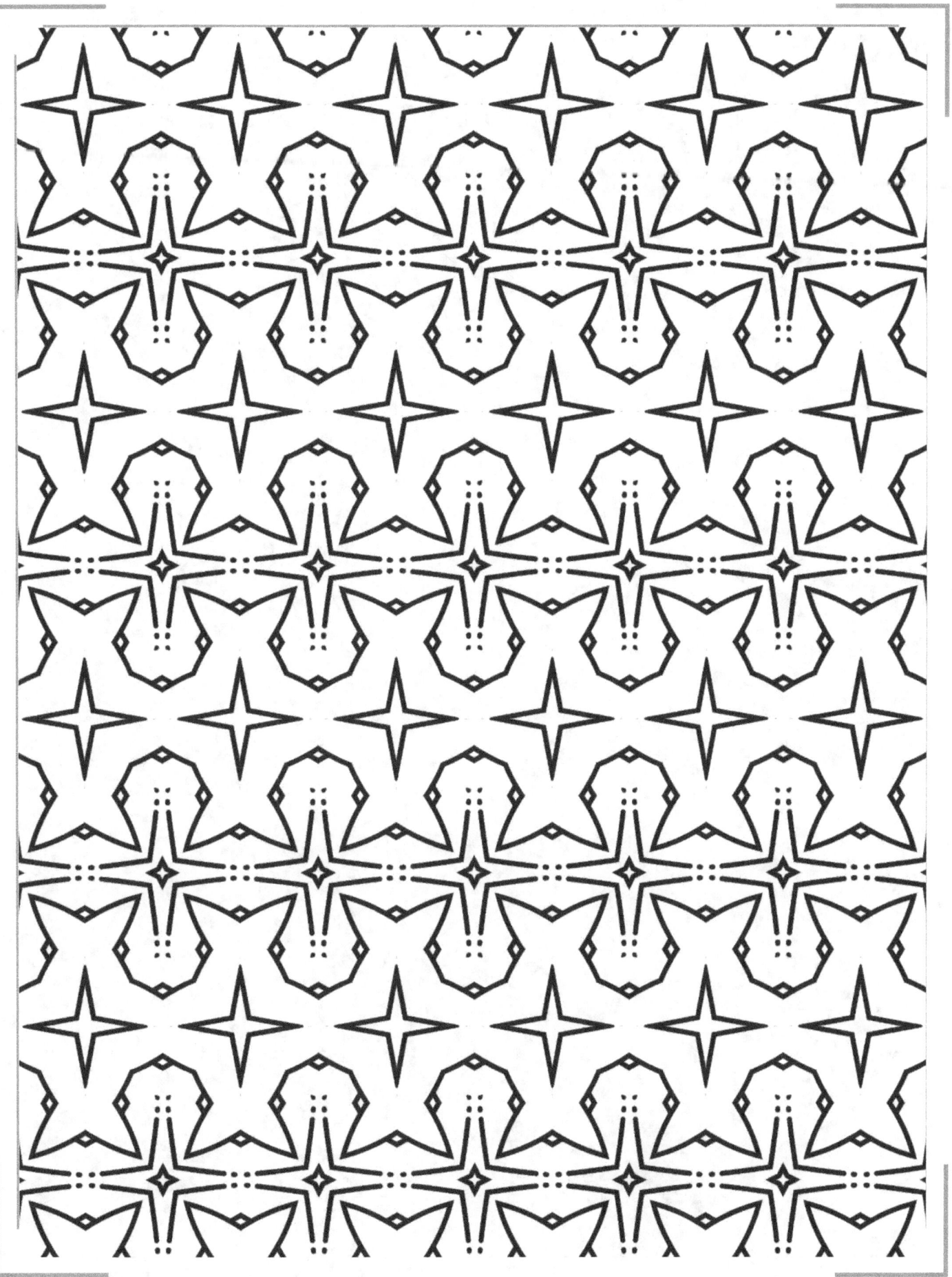

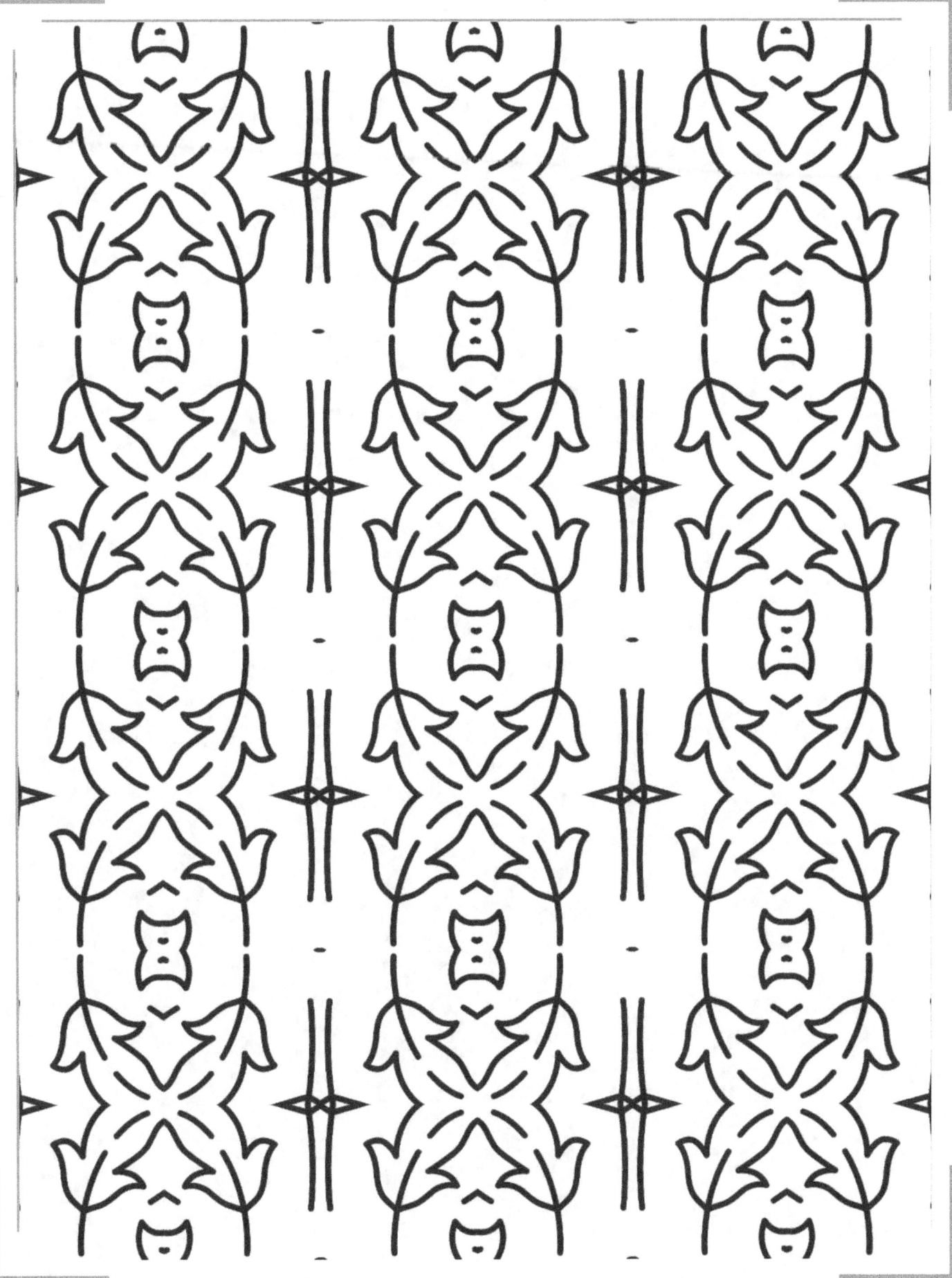

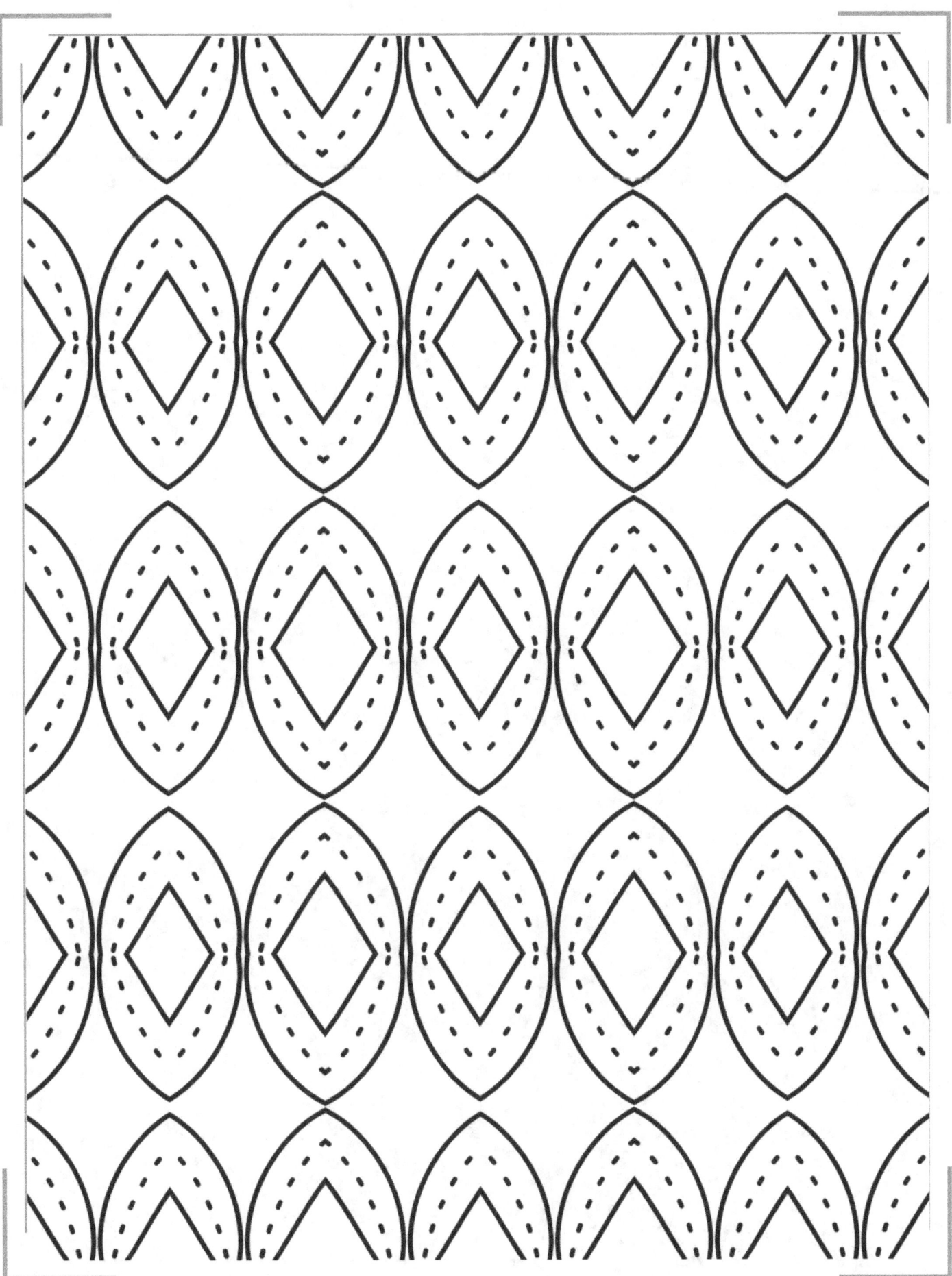

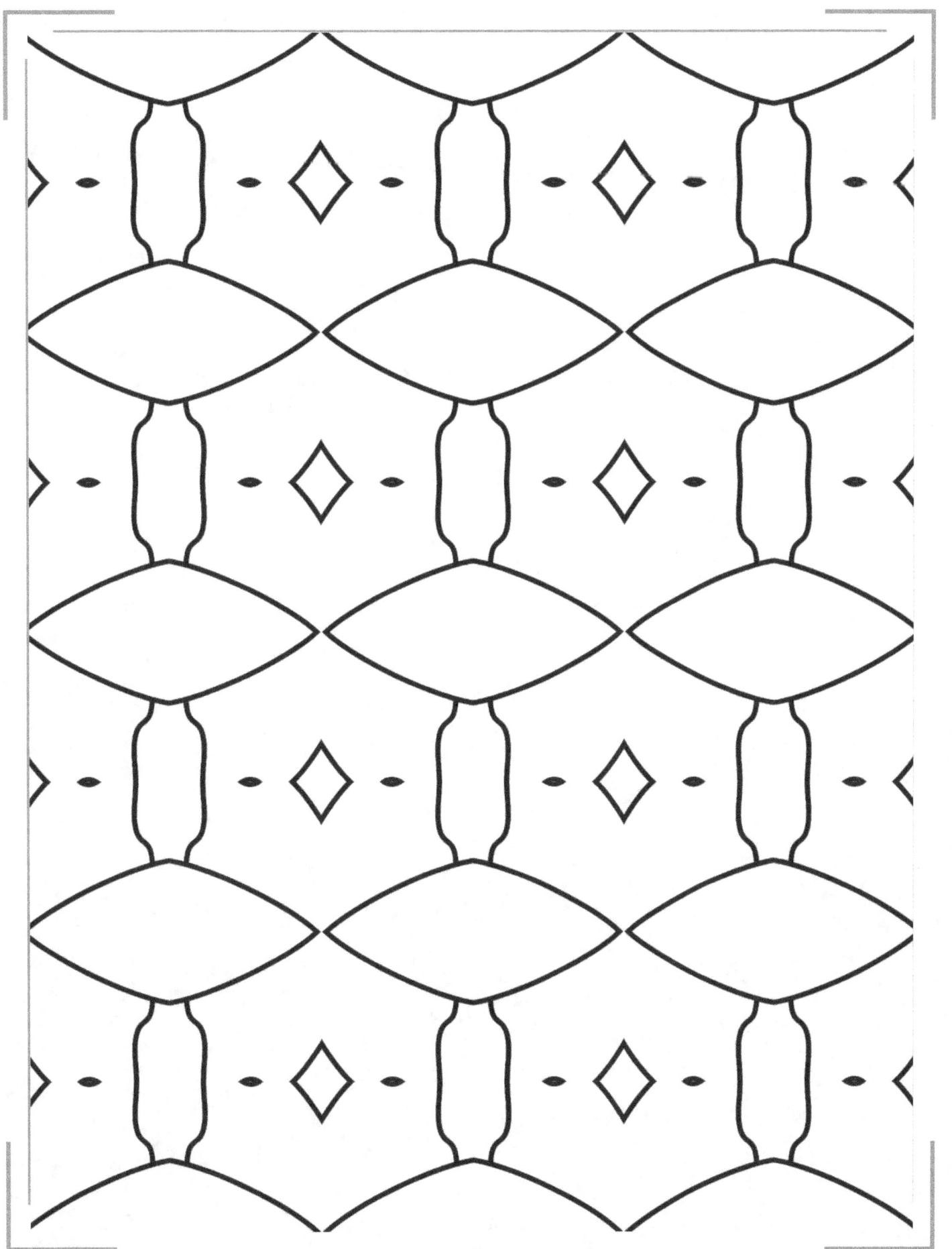

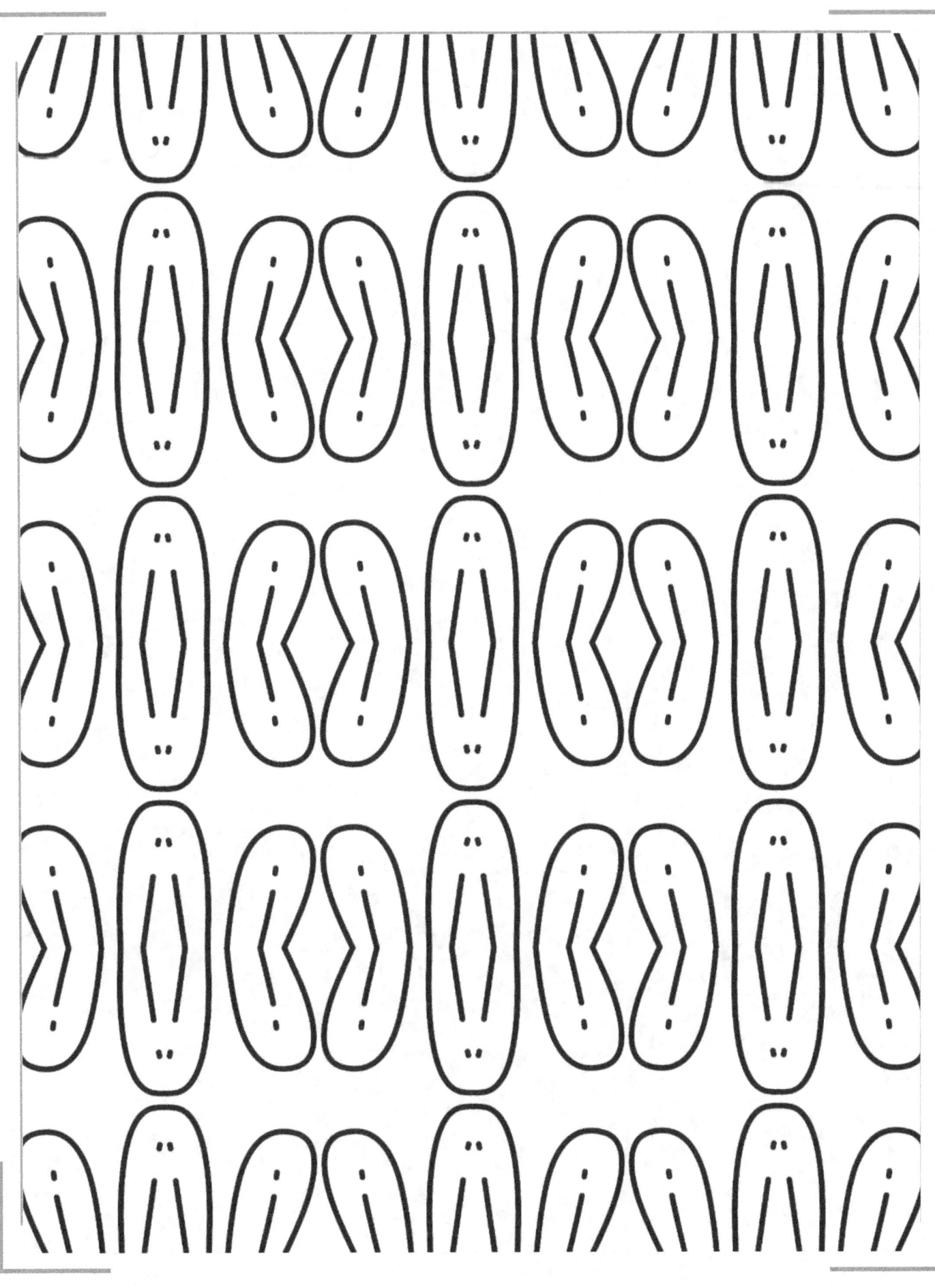

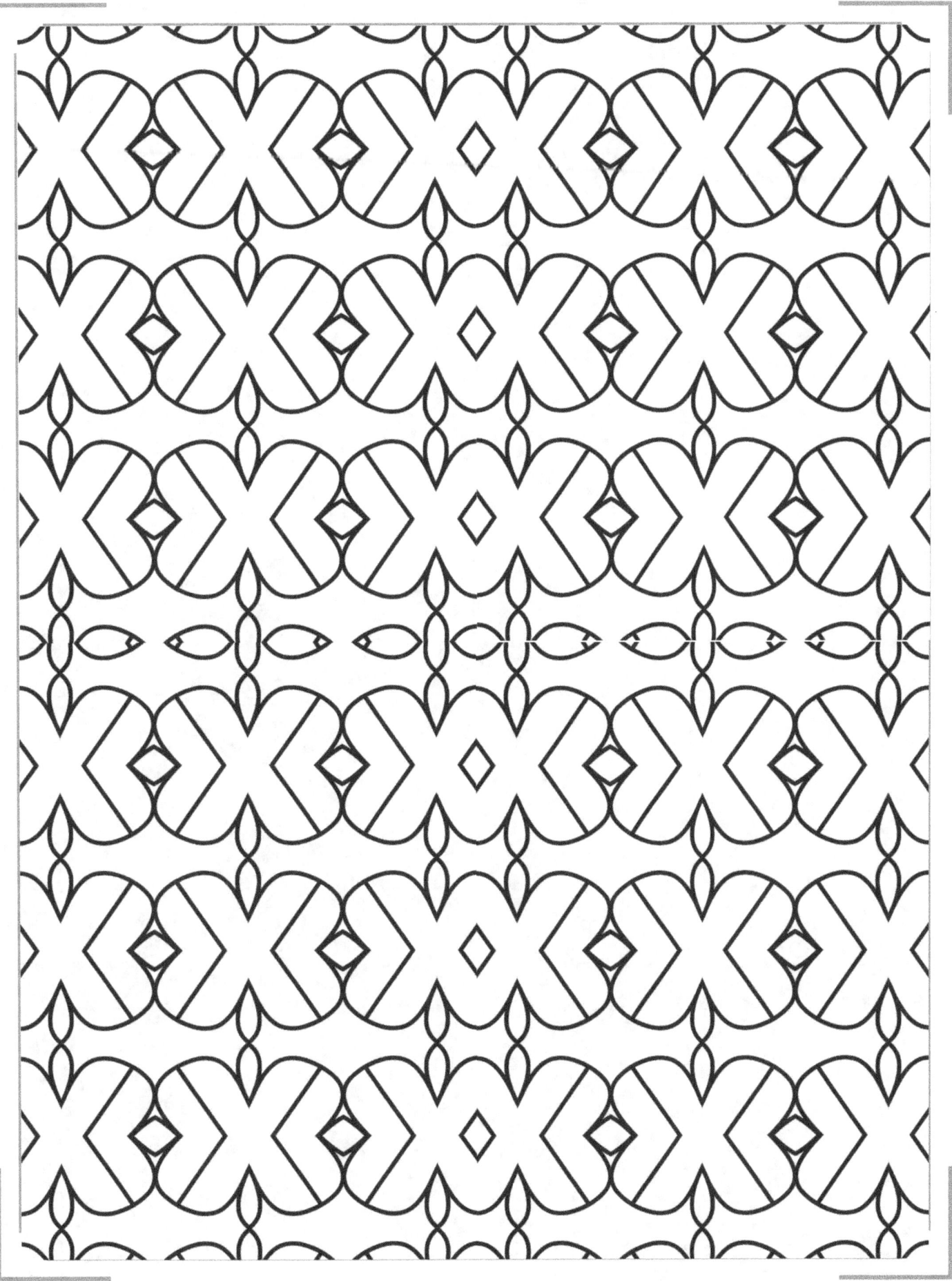

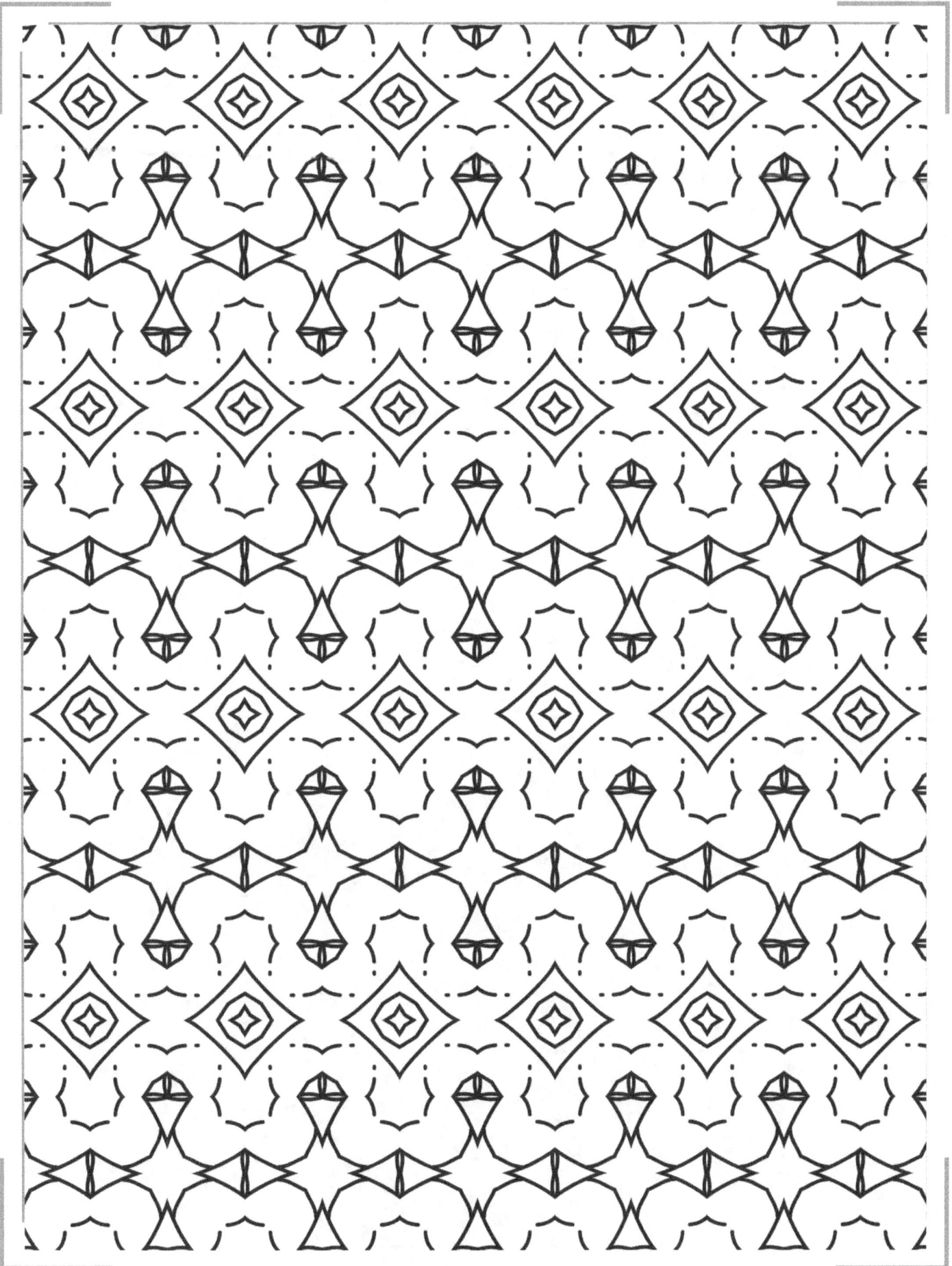

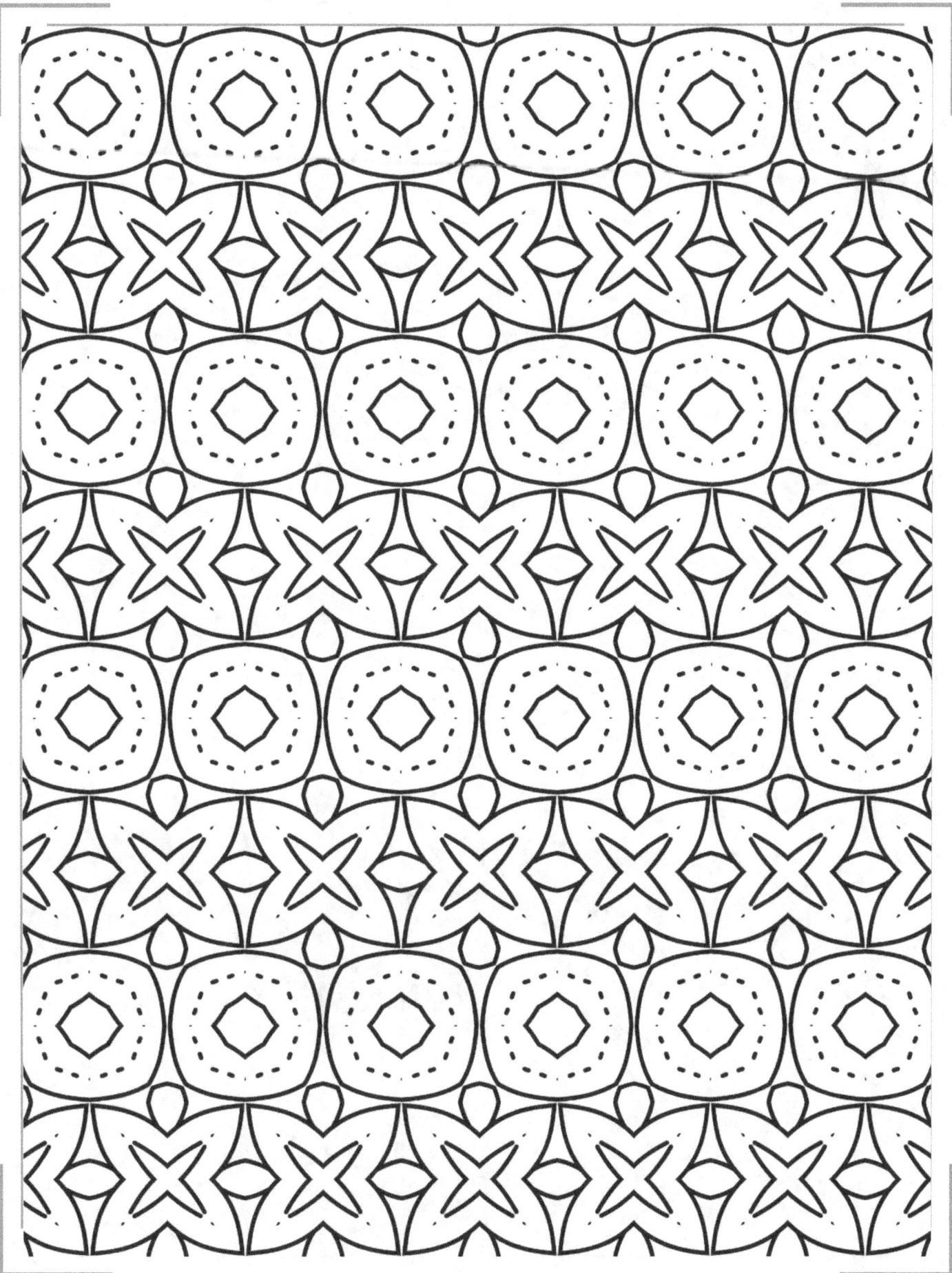

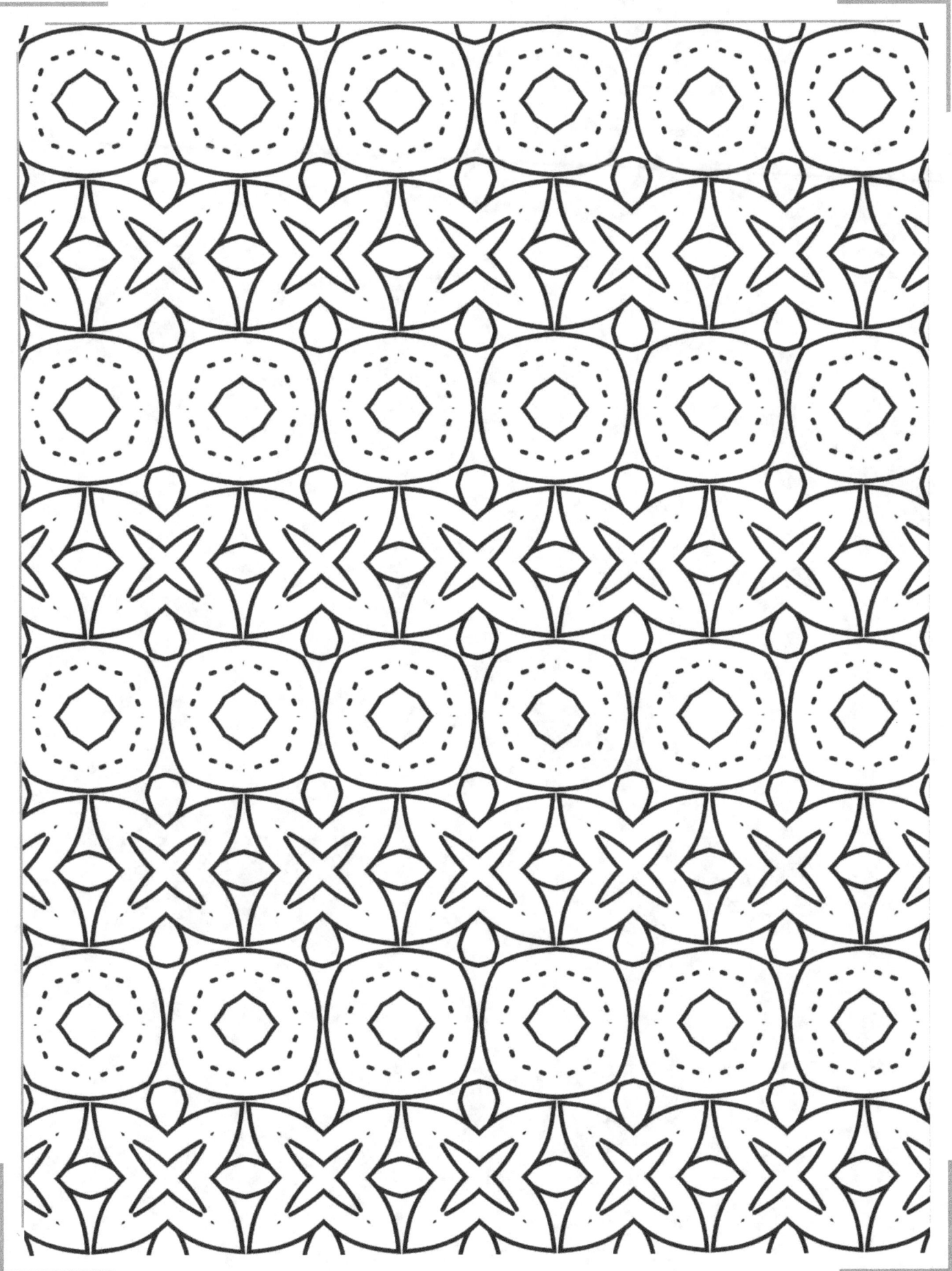

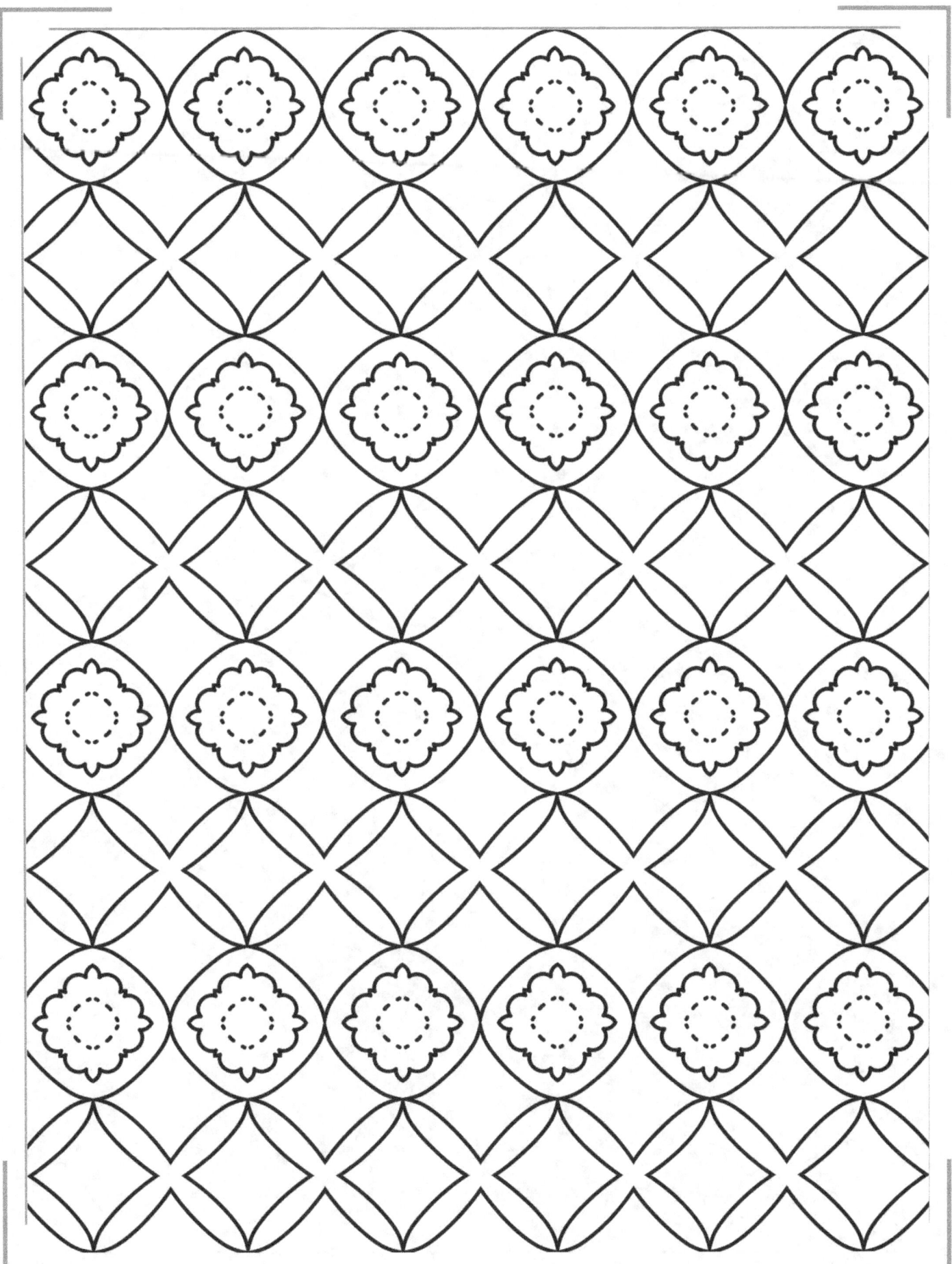

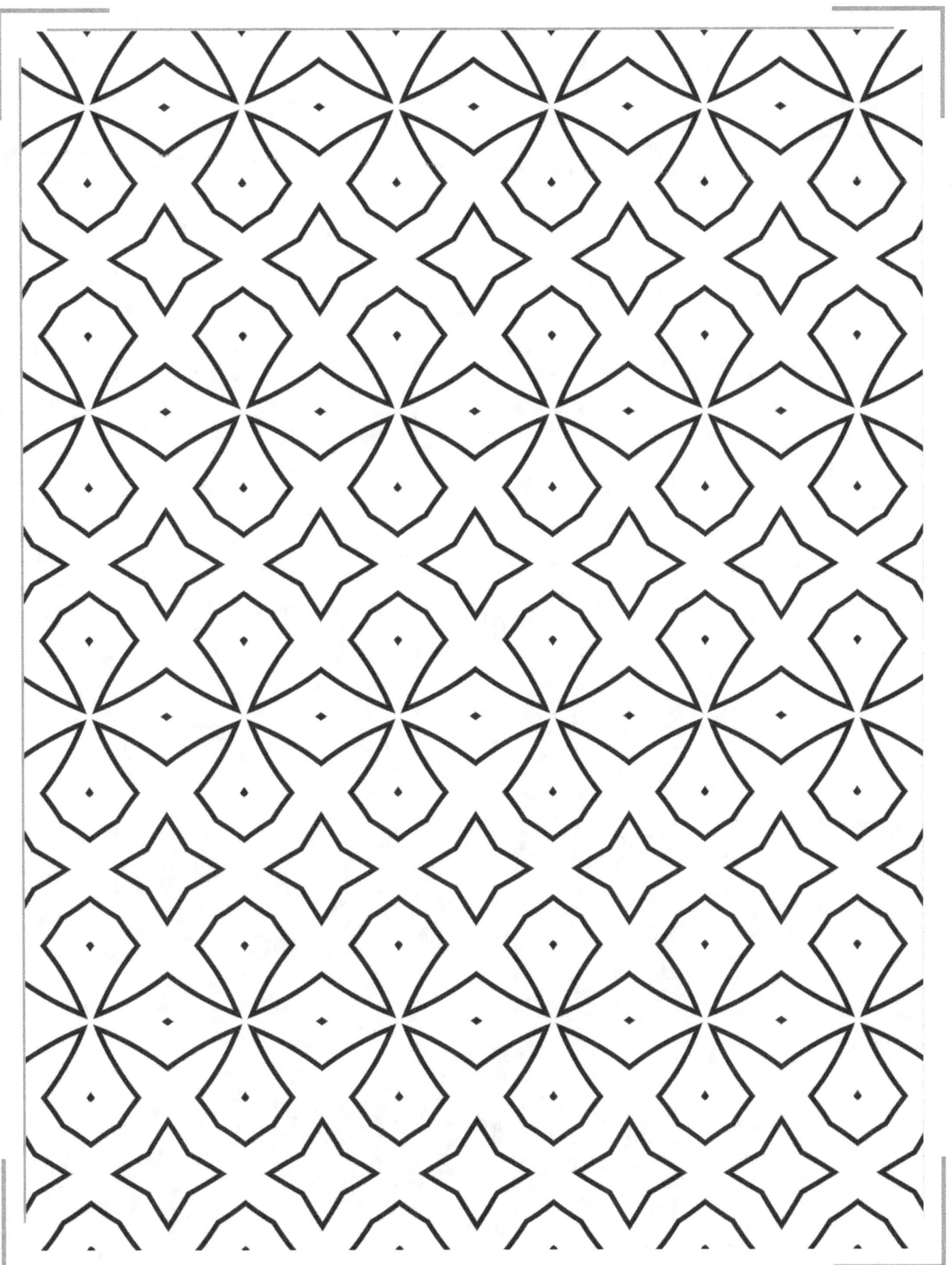

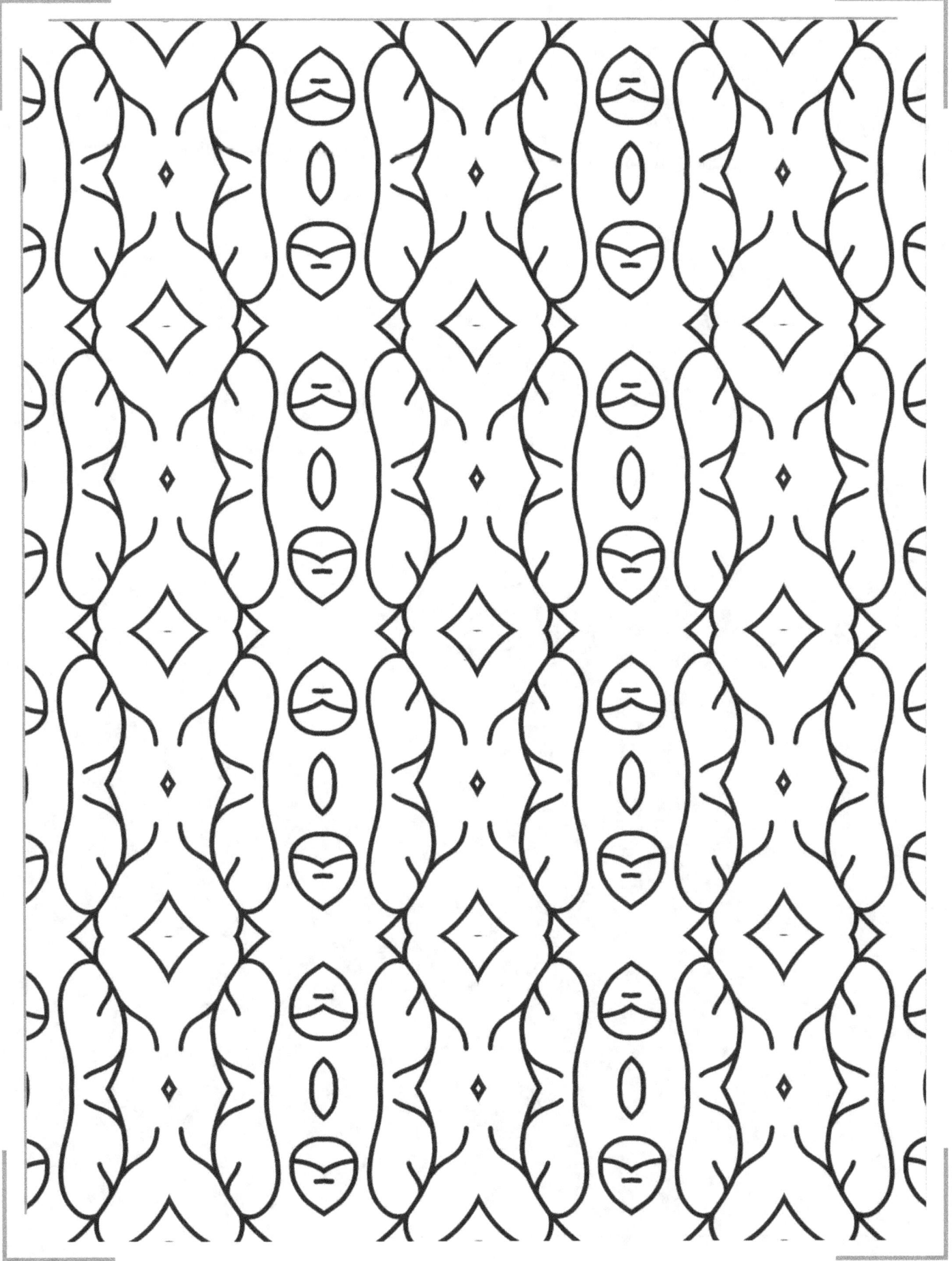

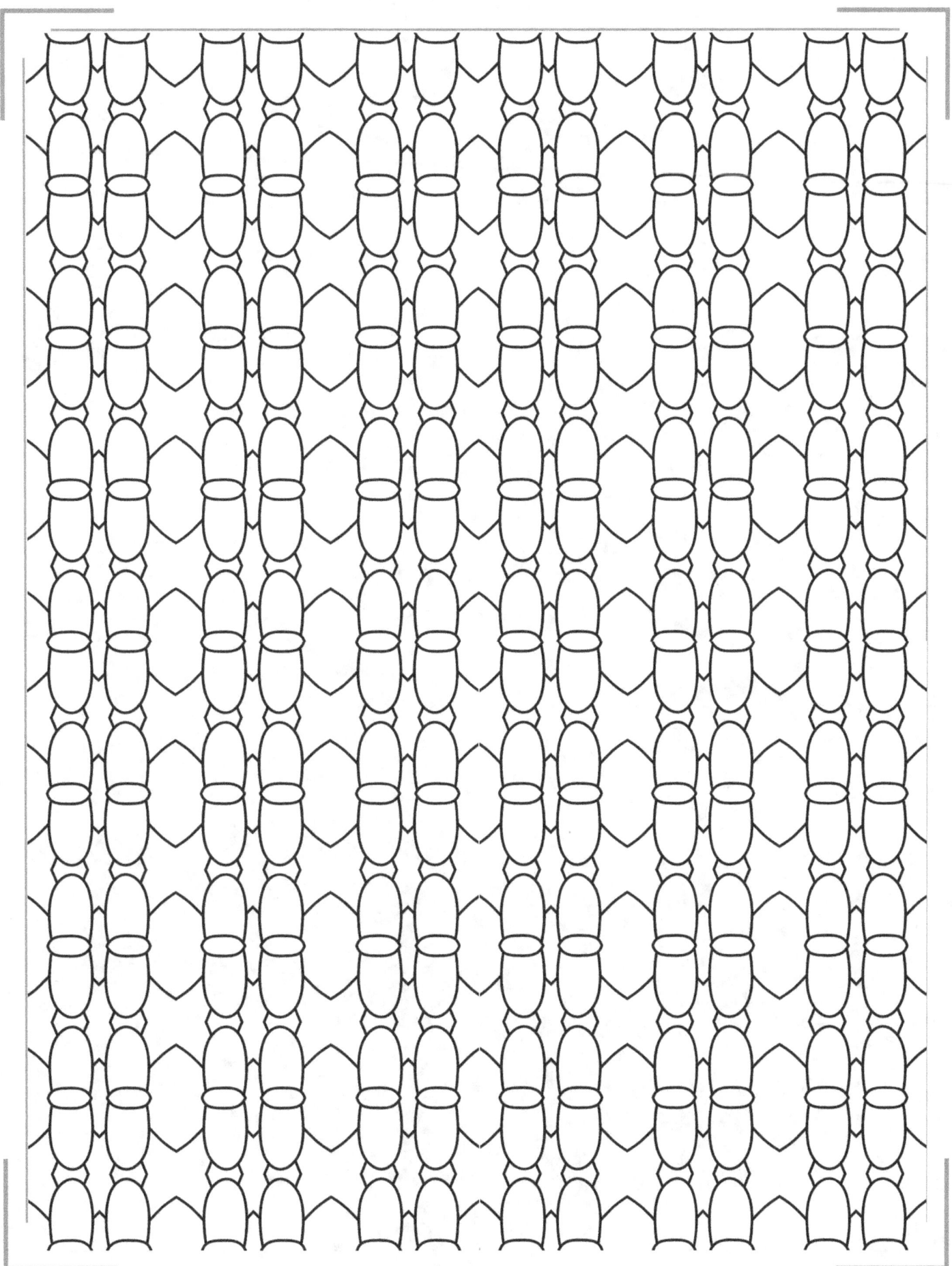

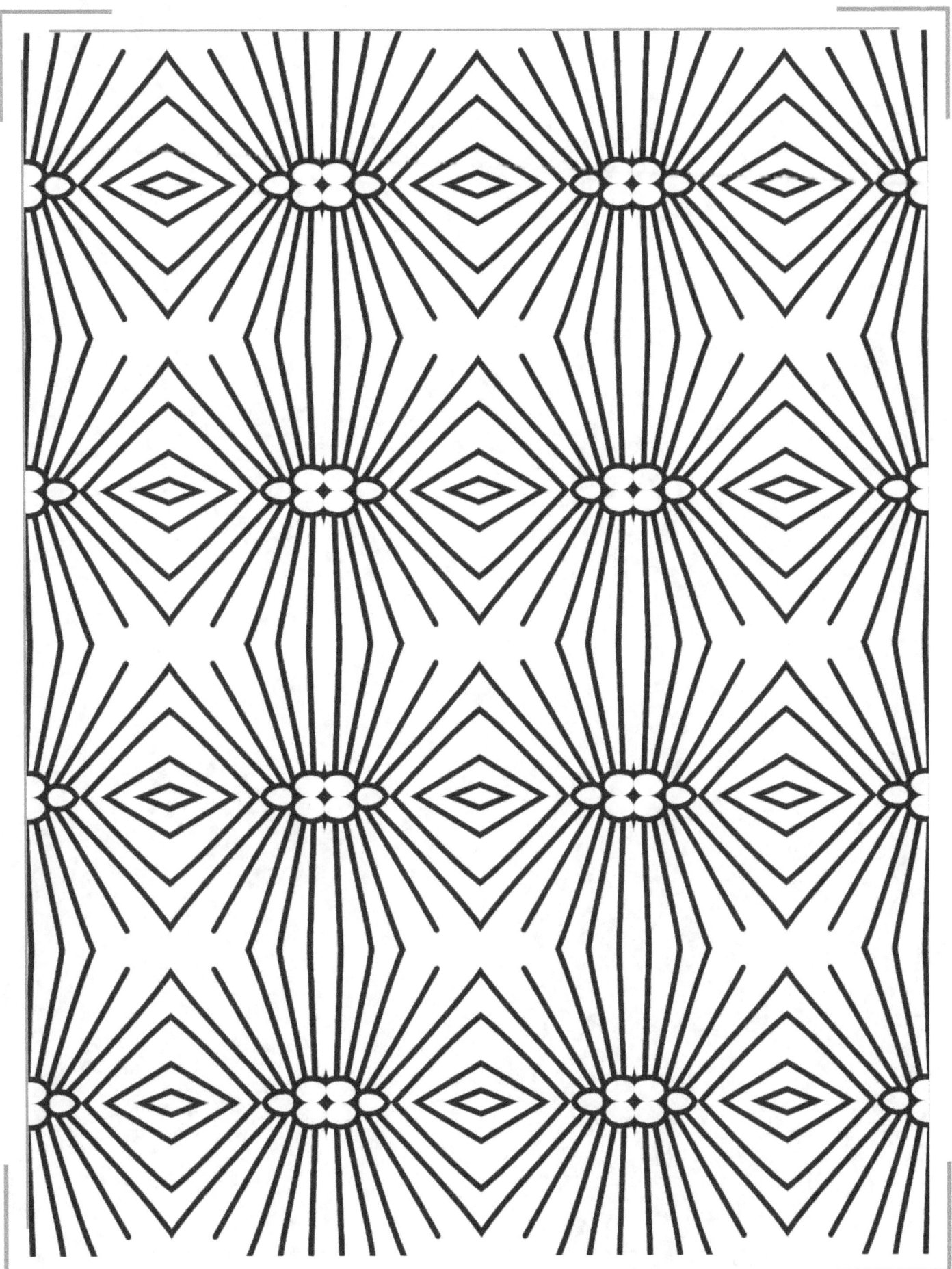

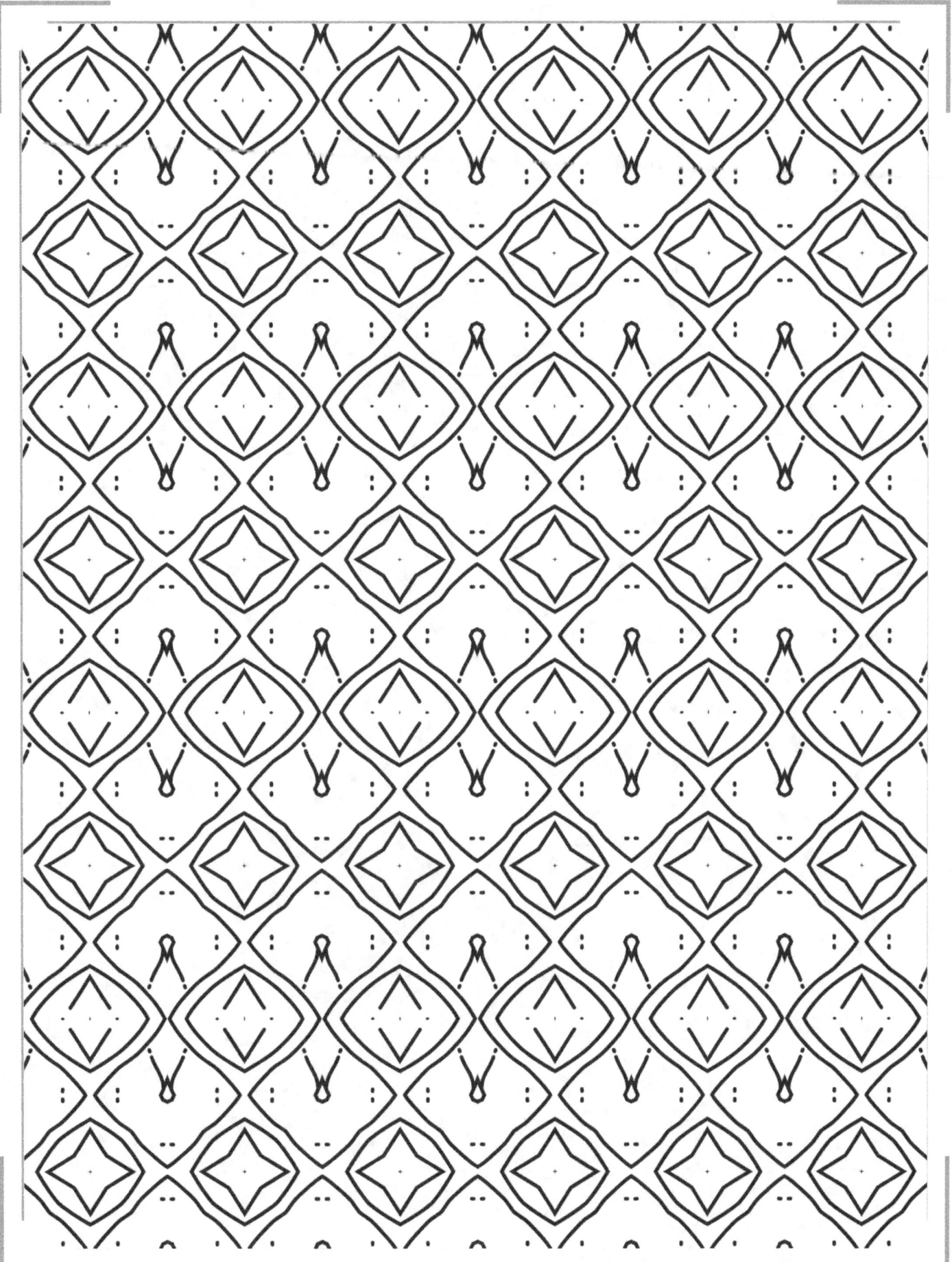

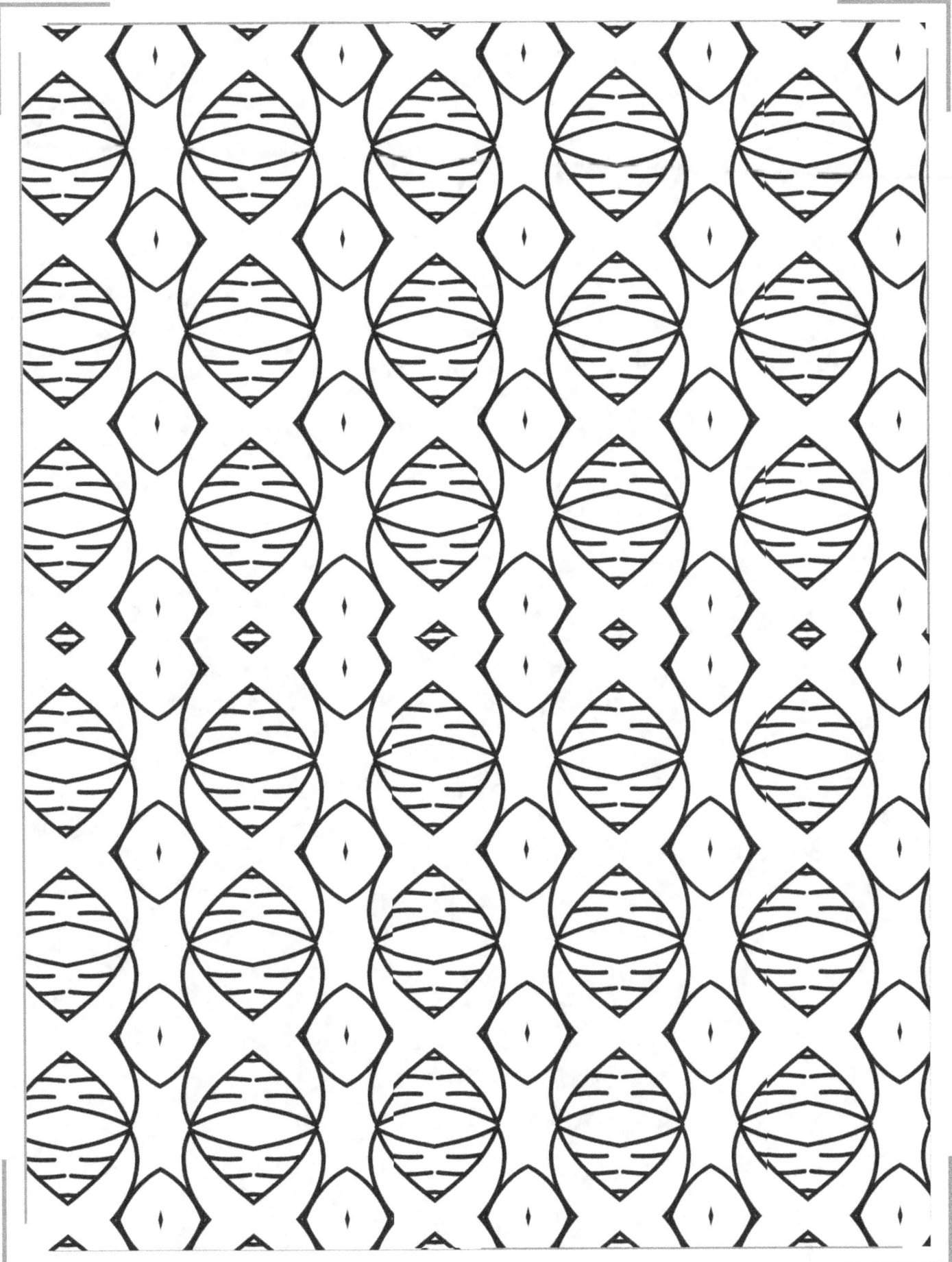

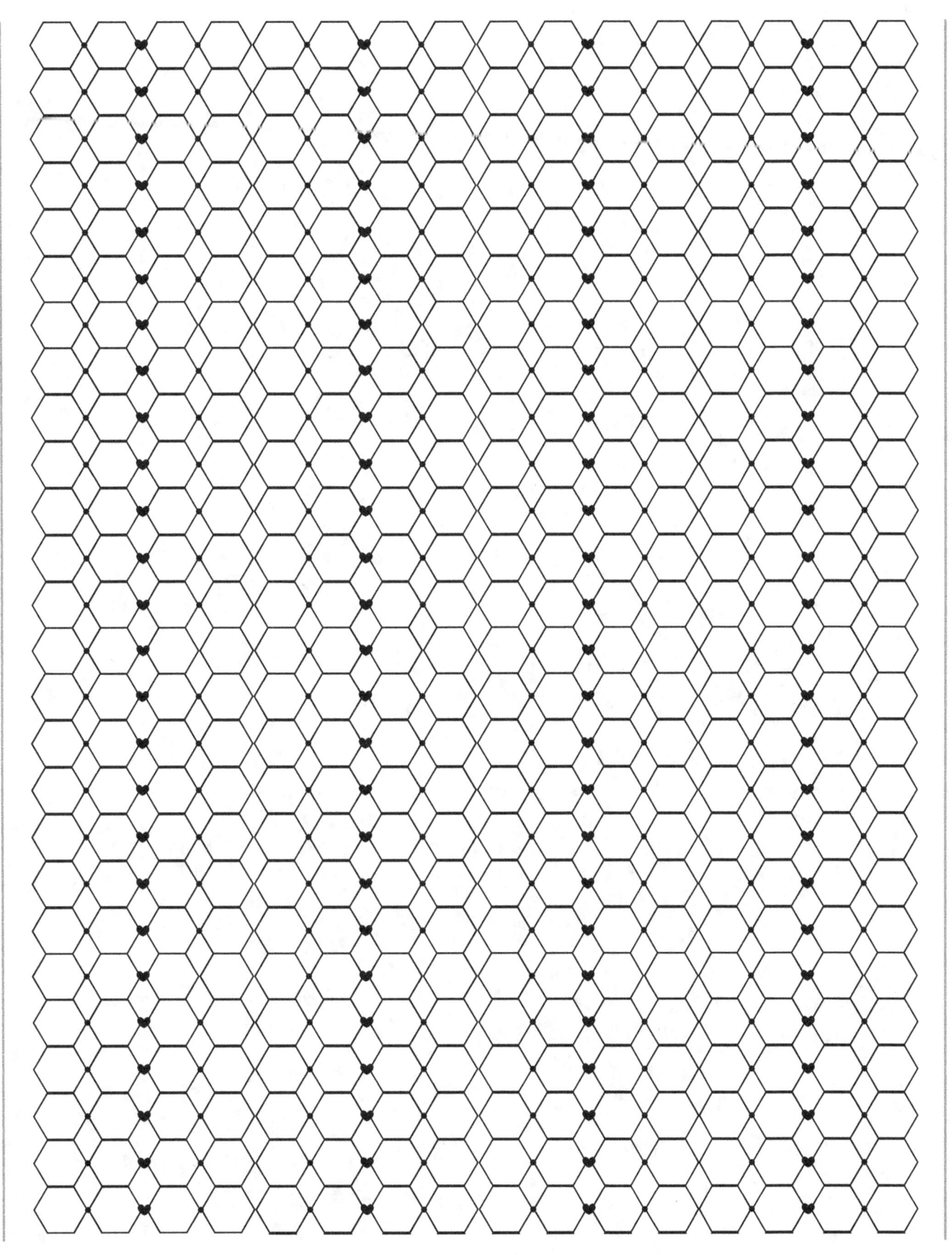

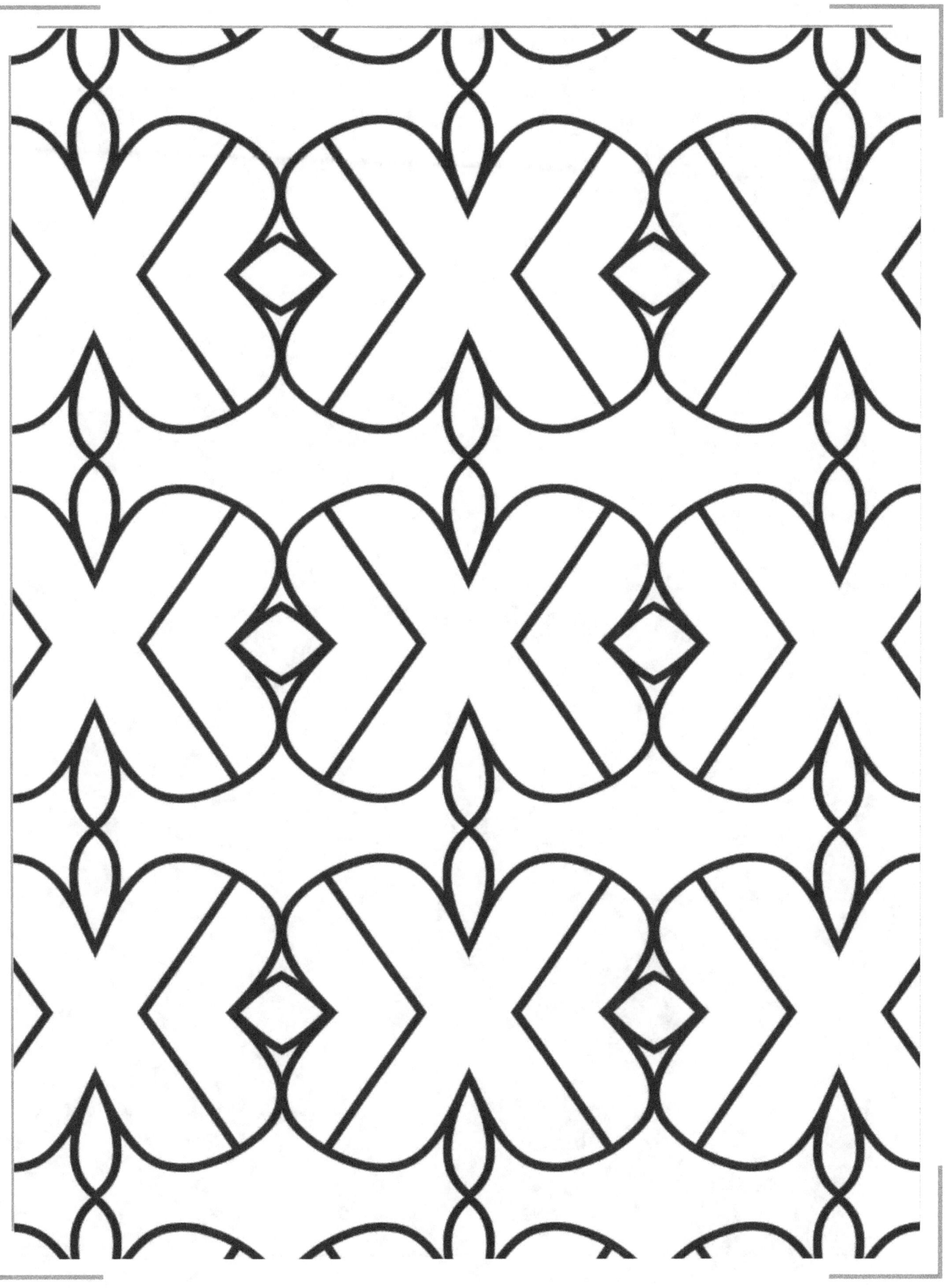

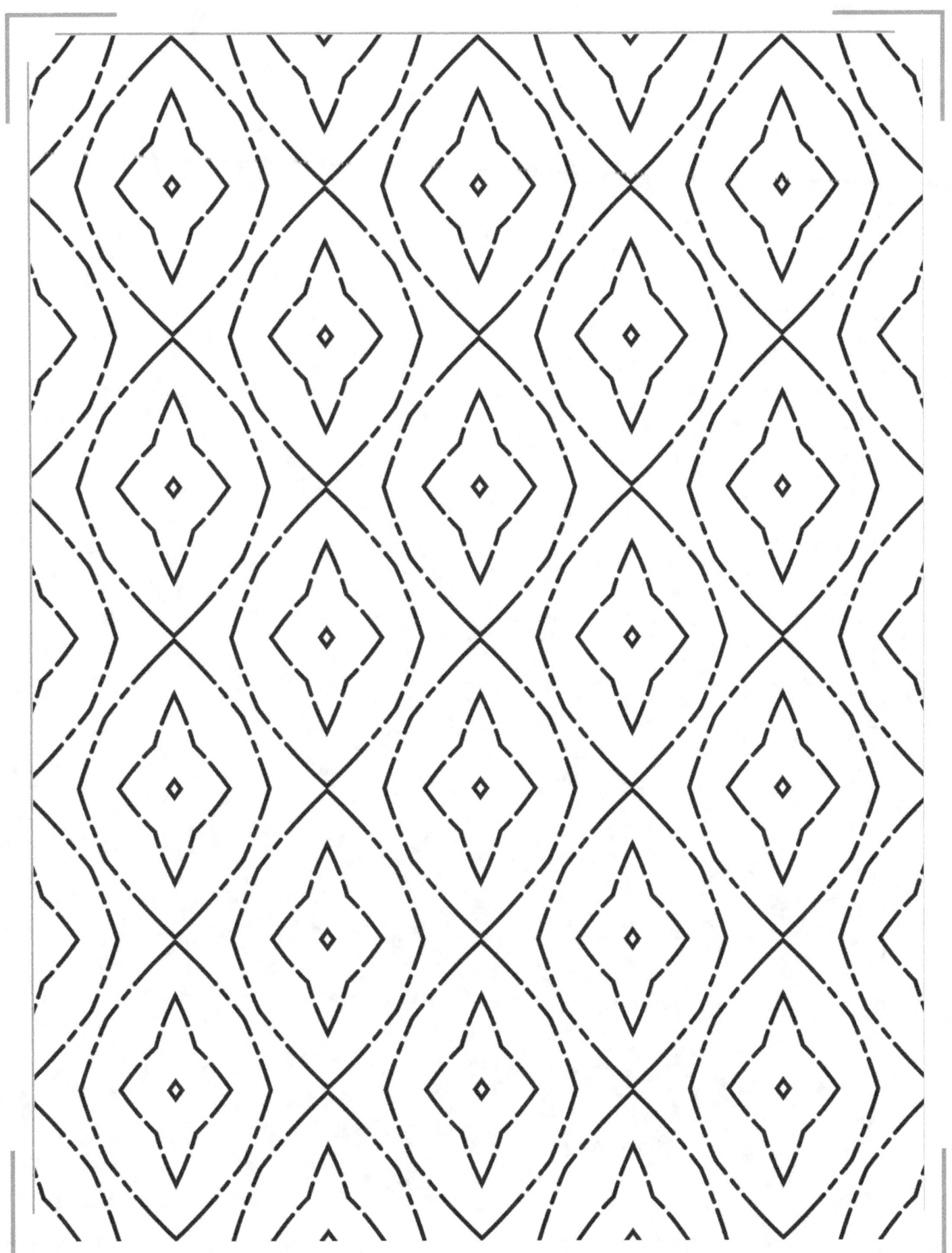

BONUS PAGE

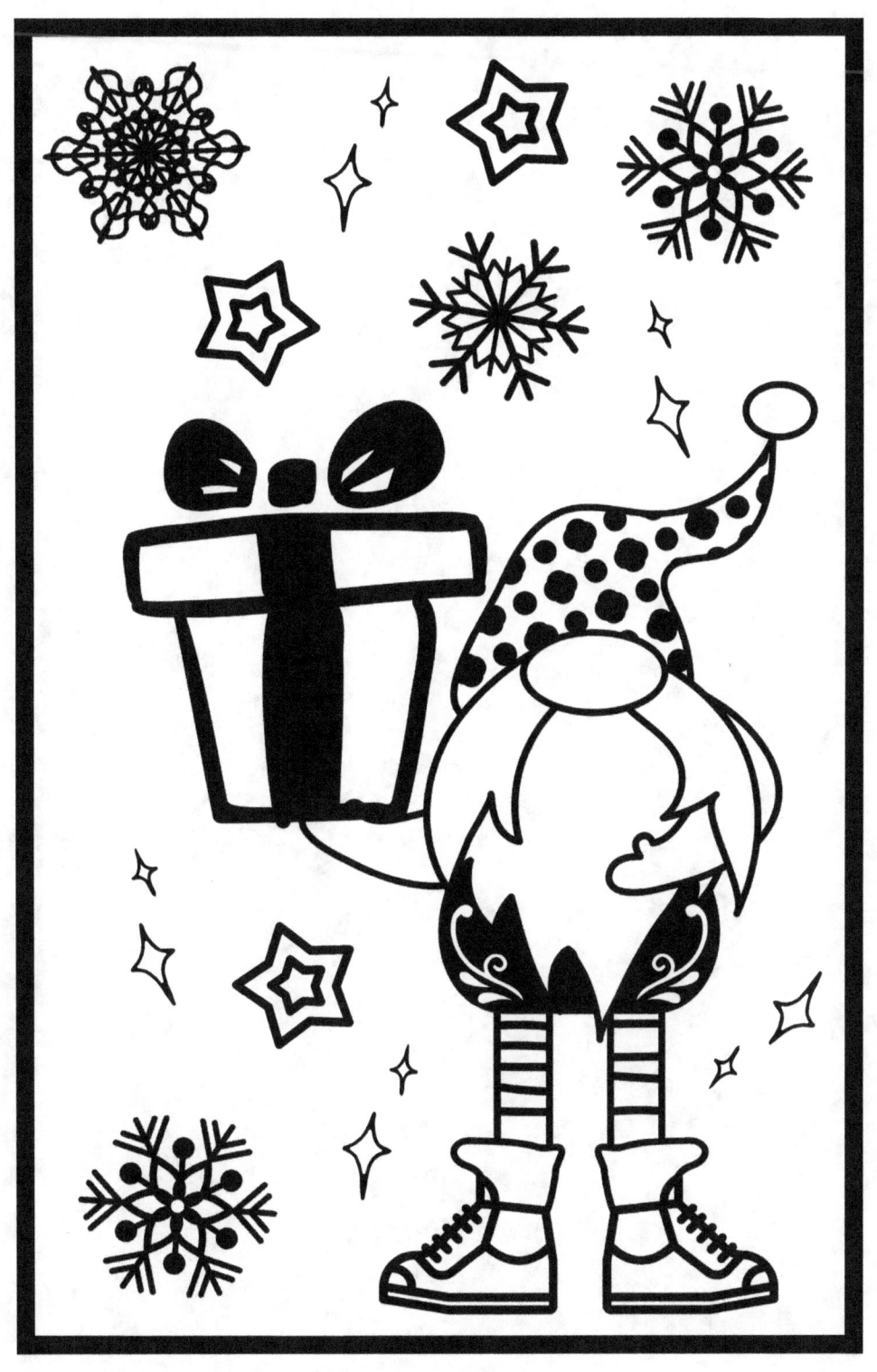

More in: "Christmas Gnomes Coloring Book"

BONUS PAGE

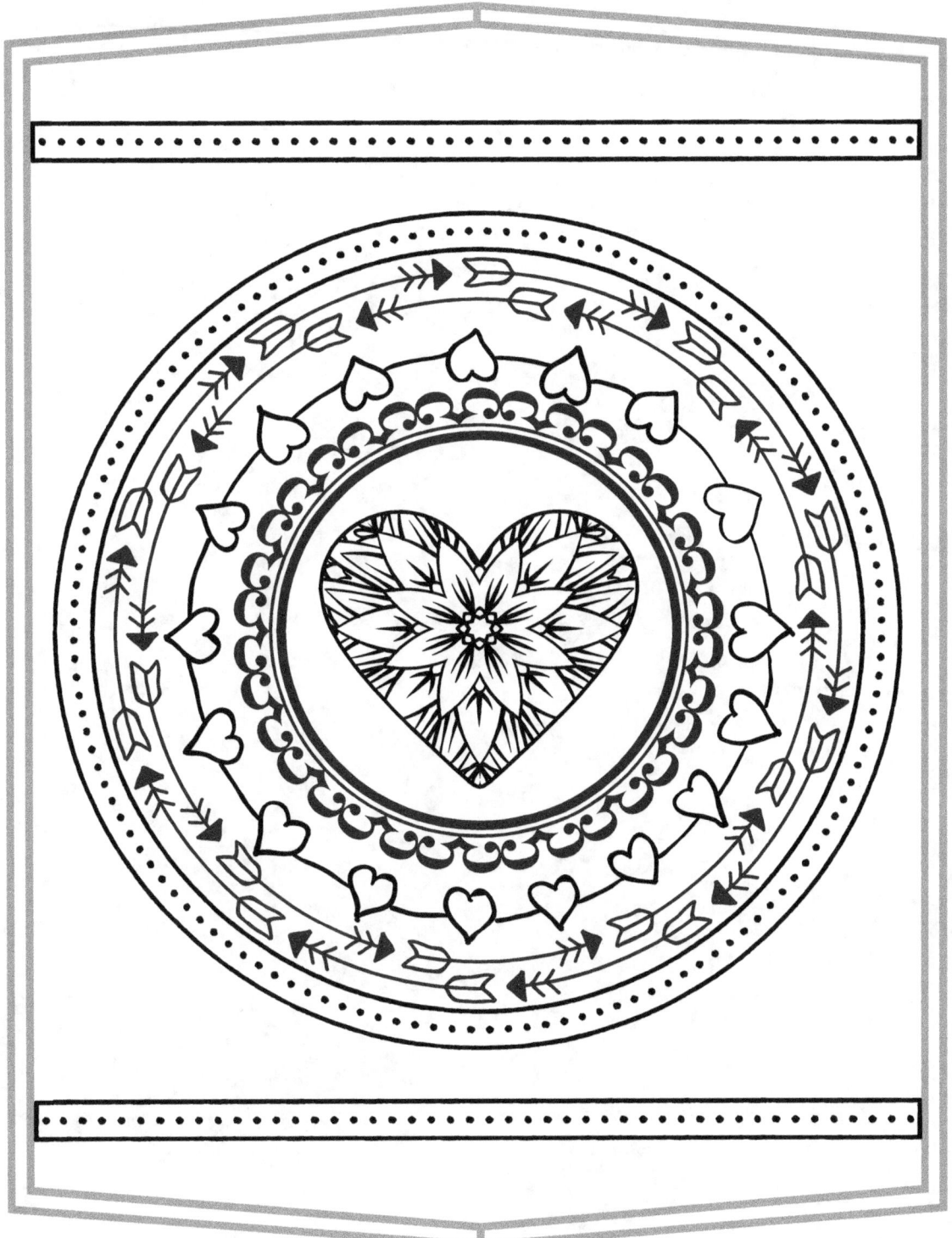

More in: "Romantic Mandalas Coloring Book"

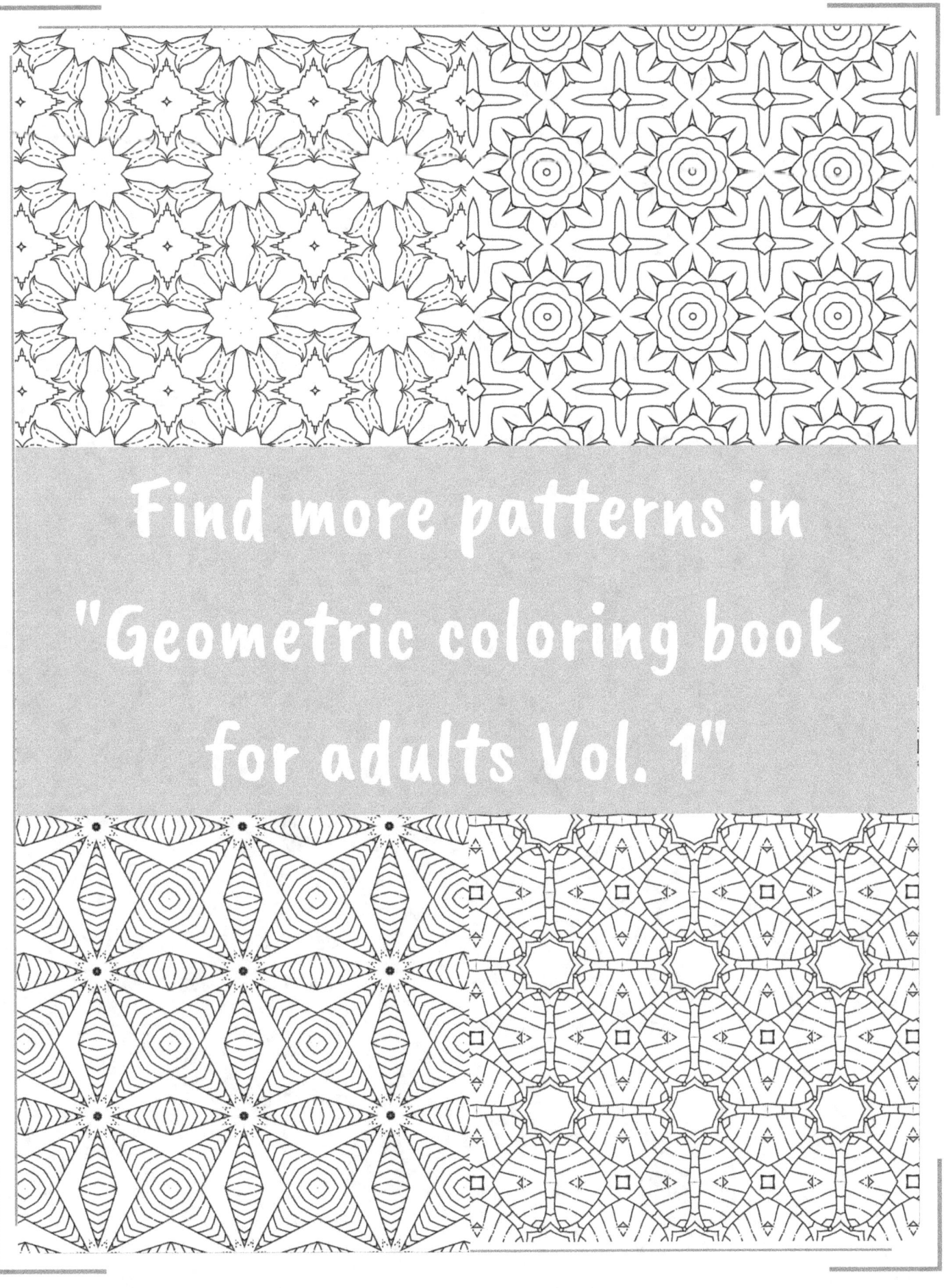

www.ingramcontent.com/pod-product-compliance
Lightning Source LLC
Chambersburg PA
CBHW080555220526
45466CB00010B/3154